A Survivor's Surrender

Healing One Layer at a Time

Jackson Hanks

A Survivor's Surrender

Healing One Layer at a Time

Jackson Hanks

Published by Tom Bird Retreats, Inc.

Cover Photos courtesy of Red Fire Grille, Palestine, Texas. Photos by LadyEm Photography; Emily Green, photographer.

Library of Congress Cataloging-in-Publication Data

For permissions:

Jackson Hanks
jackson@jacksonhanks.com
JacksonHanks.com

ISBN 0-978-1-62747-335-4 (paperback)
ISBN 0-978-1-62747-329-3 (eBook)

Dedication

To every man, woman, adolescent and child who has been abused or traumatized in any way, I dedicate this book to you.

For you to become who you truly are, I encourage you to do as I did years ago. I surrendered my ego and started dealing with the hidden emotional monsters which had controlled my life until that moment.

I encourage you to find the books that speak to you and allow yourself to embrace the knowledge and wisdom of the authors. Also, if the scars of your past are deep enough, I strongly suggest you find the right professional counselor, therapist or psychologist to work with.

Should you do so, my wish for you is that you find the professional who will help you find the lessons chasing you, help you deal with the pain they've brought into your life, and guide you through the healing process so you may put them to rest.

Imagine living in a world where you, your family and friends live as your true and authentic selves.

Gratitude

Sara Hays

Sara is a Licensed Clinical Social Worker (LCSW) in Winnsboro, Texas, who specializes in family-of-origin issues. In my humble opinion, her assessment skills and wisdom are beyond compare.

As I tell folks, don't worry about Sara hitting the target - she'll tell you what's in the *bull's-eye* of the target. For me, her wisdom is off the charts!

Here is a link to her profile:

www.psychologytoday.com/us/therapists/sara-r-hays-winnsboro-tx/74302

Renee Bouma

Renee is a Licensed Transformational Coach, Certified Hypnotist and Reiki Master. She also does amazing intuitive energy work. In addition, she is my business partner in work we do called "The Soul of You."

Renee has incredible insight and wisdom, plus she meets you where you are. Her intuitive energy sessions are some of the most amazing hours I've had on planet Earth. Not only does she run energy in those sessions at a level I've known only her to reach, she always gives you powerful information. Her insights go beyond amazing and are always are spot on!

www.reneebouma.com

Judy Goodman

Judy is an amazing intuitive, life coach, clairvoyant, recovery coach, hypnotherapist and more. She gifts her clients and students with wisdom beyond conventional thinking, taking you to personal levels you never realized were possible in your life. I can personally vouch for that, as she has helped me become my authentic self from the shell of a man I was when I first met her.

www.judygoodman.com

Frankie Burget

Frankie practices under her trade name Windsong Therapy, in Bedford, Texas. Her patients come from word-of-mouth referrals as well as from physicians, chiropractors and surgeons who can't solve their patients' issues. Frankie's knowledge of human anatomy and healing processes for the human body is incredible. I found her skills to be incomparable. She has helped me get rid of emotional energies stuck in my body from childhood, as well as to release physical pain from my body. Frankie is not only well trained, but is highly intuitive as well.

windsongtherapy.com

Edith Mitchell

Edith is a certified Natural Health Professional, Master Herbalist, Doctor of Naturopathy, and has been an Iridologist/ Stress Management Practitioner for over thirty years. She has worked with numerous title company employees, and me. We've all become healthier because of her assessments and recommendations. Her iridology work is uncannily accurate, and her stress management techniques helped me rid myself of psychological wounds I had held onto.

Meet My Practitioners

For a short video from each of the above-mentioned practitioners, please go to my website, jacksonhanks.com and click on the tab "Meet Jackson."

Thanks to technological advances, all my practitioners are able to work by distance sessions.

Warning!

Some of my childhood story is beyond shocking - even to me as an adult. As a child I was trapped by my parents, with no path to safety. My psychological therapist told me that by age four I had developed PTSD (Post-Traumatic Stress Disorder).

The events I write about in this book are from my memory, my recollection. It is likely you will find some of the details to be graphic, repulsive and horrific. They were to me as an adult in recovery, and still are.

At an early age the seeds of shame, guilt, embarrassment, "can't get it right," "not good enough," "it's always my fault," and more, were sown inside me - thanks to what I endured. Those seeds could be the same ones you have, even though they look different to you.

The road to recovery is different for each of us.

This is my journey. I share it with the deepest hope that some small bit of my truth, lessons learned, and wisdom gained might enlighten your journey in some way.

As mature adults, we must have the heart to see abuse when it happens and have the resolve to help those who feel there is no hope.

Note: The stories in this book are all true, but the names have been changed in some circumstances to protect privacy.

Testimonials

This is a very powerful – and a bit frightening – account of the effect that child abuse can have on the entire life of a person, even deep into adulthood. Jackson has done a sterling job of recording his deep inquiry of recovery from a totally traumatic childhood of physical, verbal, emotional, ritual, sexual, and psychological abuse.

Recovery has been a long, hard road for him – and he shares his journey with honesty, and compassion for others, like him, who are also on the path.

While his story is sometimes horrific, he concludes with bright rays of light that can help others, and I commend him for not yielding to the darkness he describes.

Bill Worth - Editor, and author of the novels:

- House of the Sun: A Metaphysical Novel of Maui
- The Hidden Life of Jesus Christ: A Memoir
- Outwitting Multiple Sclerosis: How Forgiveness Helped Me Heal My Brain by Changing My Mind.

Jackson is the most courageous man I've ever worked with. He explored a childhood of horrendous abuse and offers hope and healing to others as he described his own recovery path.
Sara R. Hays, LMFT, LCSW.

I enjoyed our relationship so much when I was the Texas Department of Transportation's District Engineer in Tyler, Texas, and appreciated Jackson's help in the Transportation Program. He was an outstanding recipient of the Texas Road Hand award.

Bobby Evans, P.E.

I had a major (huge!) breakthrough during one section of the book. Plus little epiphanies throughout - which are as important! This book was very relatable for me and no doubt will help others. I could go on!

Janet Franecki - Proofreader.

Jackson's book is transparent and deeply moving. It is filled with encouragement, motivation, and sprinkled with humor. I'd say a must read for anyone who has been abused or traumatized.

As a mental health professional, working with victims of sexual, physical and emotional trauma, I found the book to show amazing strength through a journey many people would never share for fear of disbelief, rejection or sheer avoidance of buried memories.

This book is written from the heart and one you will want to re-read many times.

Charlene McCauley-Mayfield M.A., LPC.

Contents

Author's Note

This book is NOT about me, but instead is about my life experiences, lessons learned and wisdom gained through my healing process.

Chapters offer hope, encouragement and bits of wisdom that could help you deal with what has been holding you back from becoming the best you can be!

Jackson Hanks

1

A Rubber Glove Surprise

Several years ago, I scheduled a physical exam with my family practice doctor, David Thompson. The physical occurred a few years after I had completed intense "child within" recovery work.

I knew David well, as he was two years behind me in school, both of us having grown up in Palestine, Texas. Plus, for a time as adults we shared a passion for playing golf, at which he was very good.

Steve Presley, a well-known pharmacist in town, told me that David was highly respected in his field and had a great deal of common sense. Plus, he was practical, had an excellent bedside manner and looked out for his patients' best interests instead of his own pocket book.

I was healthy as a horse, as we say in East Texas, and had no reason to believe there would be any surprises during the exam. Until the last part of the exam, the rubber glove check of my prostate, there weren't any.

David used his fingers to discern if he could feel any abnormalities in that organ. That part of the exam was uncomfortable to me, which I accepted as normal. David wrapped up the exam and told me everything looked good so far.

What he didn't know was that I was biting my upper lip as hard as humanly possible without breaking the skin. That helped me hold back the dam full of tears waiting to roll down my cheeks.

David's rubber glove exam hit an emotional trigger I didn't realize still existed. I believed I had released them all during my child within recovery work with Sara Hays.

Once David left the room, all I wanted to do was to crawl into the space between the wall of the exam room and the next room over. I NEVER, EVER wanted to be seen again by anyone. Period.

I put my clothes on, still deeply shaken. Then I left the doctor's office, saying as few words as possible.

Sara was the amazing psychologist whom I had worked with in my child within recovery work. At the time, she had offices in Dallas and Winnsboro, Texas. She had taught me that most victims of sexual assault do their best to avoid having their pictures taken. Yet this wanting to vanish from human sight on planet Earth was new to me.

It wasn't just in the doctor's office that I didn't want to be seen.

I did not want to be seen by anyone ever again.

In retrospect, I had internalized the guilt, shame and embarrassment of being sexually assaulted. I did so by making the assaults be my fault - even though they began at age three.

That's what most survivors do. Plus, it was the loss of the innocence of youth that I've carried forward with me to the present.

The next day was a work day, so I put on my mask of happiness and managed to pull off a normal day. No one at the office noticed my emotional state. But there had been an enormous shift within me.

To get past this milestone event took time, even with the substantial skills I had gained during years of working with a range of professionals and doing extensive child within work. Emotional wounds from being sexually assaulted always cleared at their own pace for me. I had already learned that they usually cleared in layers.

Unbeknownst to me at the time, my emotional onion had just peeled off another layer, exposing a deeper level of the damage I had suffered as a child.

Those of us reliving our childhood experiences in order to clear the emotional charge behind the dammed-up feelings from being sexually assaulted, traumatized and abused, desperately need emotional support and understanding.

A simple word of kindness, compassion, understanding or caring can have a powerful impact on a survivor. Those I received are remembered, and made a difference in my life at the time. A hug from someone who says, "I care," would be a warm, protective blanket for a sexual assault survivor who had their inner light and youthful innocence stolen by monster perpetrators.

Only a survivor of sexual abuse can understand the value a new stuffed animal or blanket holds. For me, having Rabbit to hold onto at night made a great difference, as you will learn later.

Many people shy away from victims of sexual assault. That could be because they fear there is something wrong with the victims themselves. They needn't be afraid - survivors don't ask others to take on their emotional trash.

We simply seek compassion, understanding, love and encouragement. The battles we have to fight are ours alone to deal with.

2

A Rear End Shock

A couple of years had passed since my physical exam with David. Emotionally, I was stable once again and plowing the fields of life with fervor. I was hitting targets set for the law office, title company, and personally, too.

For many years I made it a point (and still do) to attend the Texas Land Title Institute. It's an annual seminar put on by the Texas Land Title Association, of which Texas First Title Company and I are members. I've attended something like sixteen of the last seventeen of their seminars.

All the Institutes I attended were held at the Hyatt Hill County Resort in San Antonio. From my perspective, the Institutes have the best topics and speakers each year. Plus I earn continuing education hours from the State Bar of Texas and the Texas Department of Insurance. Those hours help me keep my continuing education hours current.

That year, I was in a comfortable, well-known setting. I also knew a fair number of participants and speakers at the seminar.

The morning after checking in, I started my normal morning bathroom routine. Then it happened.

It felt like a long, sharp, jagged shard of glass was sliding sideways through my rectum.

Its pace seemed slower than a turtle crossing the road. Sweat began pouring from my face. The physical pain caused tears to stream from my eyes.

I had no idea what had gone afoul inside my body, but knew I should go on a liquid diet immediately. But wanting to have the appearance of being "normal" like everyone else, I ate solid food meals that day.

The next morning, as my bathroom experience from the day before repeated itself, I wished I had consumed a liquid diet the day before, as guided by my intuition. Again, hot beads of sweat were rolling down my face. Then came another dose of streaming tears from the physical pain.

I learned from Dr. David Thompson, whom I went to see when I returned home, that I had something called an anal fissure. David's prognosis was a true relief, as I was amazed at how much blood had shown up in the toilet bowl those mornings.

My antenna goes on ready alert any time I am around a group of men, even if they are friends. When I first realized that trait, I thought there was something really wrong with me.

Once I recovered and re-lived video-like memories from childhood, I began to understand, realizing it was only my child within wanting to be safe. Only a sexually assaulted survivor would know that's both normal and acceptable.

The men who sexually assaulted me as a child weren't strangers, they were friends of my dad. And he wasn't innocent, at all.

When triggered, an unhealed emotional wound can erupt with physical consequences to our bodies. Mine did in unexpected ways, even though there had been no prior warning.

It helped me clear another layer. Bit by bit, I was able to forgive the perpetrators.

I prayed my best to our loving Mother God that this was my final hurdle to clear all wounds of that kind. Yet of course, it wasn't.

Healing all layers of each kind of abuse takes courage, determination, patience, vulnerability and intense desire.

3
The Loss of My Innocence of Youth

My Soul/Higher Self spoke these words to me:

> **"I cry for what you experienced in childhood, Jackson. It was unfair to you or any child. The experiences, both known and unknown to you, helped mold you into being the person you are today."**

By age four I had endured enough life experiences to have post-traumatic stress disorder (PTSD), according to Sara, my wise counselor.

Sexually assaulted - check.

Ritual abuse - check.

Physical abuse - check.

Emotional abuse - check.

Verbal abuse - check.

Psychological abuse - check.

Yet to outsiders, I was a well-dressed and polite child. Of course I was! The consequences of not being so were way too painful for my young body and mind to bear. Those who knew my parents thought I was a normal youngster.

It is a frightening thought to me that so many people who knew my parents had no idea what was going on in my home.

My dad was an independent insurance agent. According to Katherine Barrett, a former employee of his, at work he was a sweet, kind man. She also told me that in our town there are folks she refers to as "street angels and house devils." Those are people who put on a good show to others, then become abusive monsters at home.

He was active in the Episcopal Church (lay reader and adult Sunday school teacher) and contributed to our community as well. He was serving on the city council at the time of his death at the ripe old age of forty-seven.

By the time I was four, I had become the family placater. This was a survival tool for me.

It is sick that a four-year-old would do his best to deal with adult emotions coming from out-of-control parents. Of course, there were good days. I lived for those.

Honestly, I likely will never deal well with adult anger, thanks to my mom, Jackie. She taught me that anger can escalate from a raindrop to a violent, raging verbal thunderstorm in an instant.

With her outbursts came insults, shaming and degrading words. They flew out of her mouth without remorse.

Physical threats spewed freely too. As a tyke I feared they would come true. Some did.

What my mom didn't know was that the impact of her thoughts and words didn't stop at her lips. Their energy "blessed" her targets with a treasure trove to work through.

She gave me the emotional gift of clearing her junk stuck inside me, plus clearing my reactions to receiving it. I feel I've cleaned up most of it, but not yet all.

Not only was I the family placater, I had a full set of adult manners instilled within me by the age of three. The expectation of perfection was prevalent in my growing up home.

Katherine, who was nineteen years old when Jack died, told me a few years ago that she used to fuss at my dad; apparently because she thought I should be allowed to be a child rather than a child acting as an adult at age three. Of course, she didn't change my dad's mind.

A consequence of being raised that way is that it is far easier for me to bury myself in my work instead of finding ways to play as an adult. So I'm left with yet another opportunity for personal development. At least I know I'll be the better for it!

Perfection? At age thirty-five I realized that perfection, of any kind, is not attainable. Not in my law office, not at home and not in business.

It was then that I decided, with only the guidance of my own heart, to become a recovering perfectionist.

I am now a recovering perfectionist. Now when I notice that a picture, portrait or a wall hanging of any sort is as little as 1/96th of an inch off center, I muse and move on without feeling the need to straighten it.

Becoming a recovering perfectionist allowed me to ditch my inner critic. I am ashamed to say I had one back then. I learned from Sara that critics criticize, like my mother, and as I had begun to be, because they are miserable within themselves.

Being raised by perfectionist parents also "blessed" me with another condition I learned about from Sara, called performance-based self-esteem.

Katherine, who later obtained her master's degree in education, imparted another piece of wisdom to me

- performance-based self-esteem is, to her, being controlled by intimidation.

During childhood I had frequent bouts of itchy rashes. Their cause was never diagnosed, though many, many doctors had the chance to do so.

My little body frequently found itself under super stress, as I was taking on all I could. I was powerless about what happened next, and my anxiety level was horrendous.

I wouldn't wish my childhood experiences on anyone. Yet I can say with absolute certainty I could not be who I am today without them.

I lost my childhood innocence by age three.

Now, in my mind I do my best to invite my child within to go play in his sandbox with his favorite toys. Sometimes he'd rather ride his bicycle, a favorite activity of his.

I watch him, love him, and appreciate him for all the things he missed growing up. His childhood innocence was stolen from him. Now at least he knows and feels that I care for and love him as if he were my very own child.

Sara taught me the importance of sitting with my child within daily. My number one task is to give him what he didn't receive growing up. So daily I give him love, laughter, appreciation and healthy encouragement.

This is a powerful exercise for me. It takes a little time, but makes a tremendous difference as to how my day goes!

4

Cigarette Smoke

As an adult, I have always had a super-strong aversion to cigarette smoke. Many times, I wondered why. Uncle Clyde, my dad's older brother, questioned me about it many times. He thought it was a peculiar behavior his nephew shouldn't have.

It took years of work, plus digging deep into memories, to make that flashlight beam come alive. When it did, I was shown why my subconscious mind held onto the deep tears and fears of cigarette smoke. I still carry a strong repulsion to it.

My mom smoked throughout her pregnancy, so I was "blessed" with those effects in the womb. She was wound up tighter than a tin drum and was an only child. After she died I learned that many women in town didn't like dealing with her.

I have memories of being dressed up like Little Lord Fauntleroy (a slight exaggeration on my part). Many times I was taken by her to the Tea Room at the Neiman Marcus store in downtown Dallas. I remember the air in the place was stuffy. My mom was always proud to show me off, as I was the perfectly behaved son.

I vividly remember her antics and the fear she instilled in waiters there and at other restaurants. I've never sent a meal back to a restaurant kitchen. She did though, many times, for what I thought were dumb reasons. As a tyke, I had no idea how utterly miserable my mom must have been.

When I was a young boy, my dad was revered by some in my hometown for the good things he did in the community. He and his friends would have poker nights. The locations would change, as different men hosted them.

Most of the poker players were veterans of World War II, and nearly all of them smoked cigarettes. By the age of five I was threatened with cigarette burns if I didn't do as they told me.

I came out with no physical scars that could be seen by others. The emotional scars were invisible too. What I experienced during those poker games (and other times) turned out to be life-changing for me.

Those men must have been sexually frustrated at home. How else could they have done what they did to me?

I was used as a "favor" for different reasons. Sometimes it was a treat for a winning hand. Sometimes it was just a man's choice, or the luck of the draw. There were times I never knew the reason why. Regardless, it was physically painful and always made me want to be left alone and hide.

As hard as I've tried, I haven't yet been able to erase the images and tastes of the men's penises from my mind. Eventually, I know I will find a way to have the energy and memory of what it felt like to be sodomized by grown men's penises at the age of three and beyond purged from my mind, body and soul. And, of course, there was oral sex on demand as well. I will seek to have the energy and memory of those experiences removed too.

To me, cigarette smoke is the smell of death - because in smoke-filled rooms I lost the innocence of my youth, which can never be retrieved.

The men had fun, played cards, drank hard liquor and had a good ole time. The ones who won money were usually doubly happy at the end of their night. Not one of the men ever took the side of an innocent child.

Years later, I had a physical exam from Canadian Dr. Robert Makar, who had moved to town in the early 1980s. The doctor kept a full waiting room for some reason, but had wisdom and took good care of his patients.

Just as in the prior physical written about in Chapter 1, the rubber-glove treatment was the last part of the exam. At that time though, I had no conscious memories of what had happened to me in childhood.

The good doctor, now deceased, asked me if I had been sexually assaulted as a child.

"Not to the best of my knowledge," I replied. It wasn't even a faint blip on my radar back then. He then asked if there had been a surgical procedure of any kind regarding my rectum. My answer was a solid no.

Yet the doctor knew, as he asked, that there's only one of two ways my rectum could be like it was. So as an adult, I missed my first discovery clue.

Even knowing that all the perpetrators are dead now brings no solace to my body or child within, though I have done much inner work and forgiven them all.

My discovery was that cigarette smoke is one of many masks some adults use. Some masks are innocent, and others, like those in my childhood memory, are dark and scary.

I keep my child within safe by staying as far away from cigarette smoke as possible. It's one of many memories that brought horror to that little boy.

5

The Power of a Stuffed Rabbit

As an adult, I had the privilege of re-learning and remembering the power a soft stuffed toy animal has for a child.

My amazing therapist, Sara, helped me start mining memories of being sexually assaulted as a child. That proved to be an enormous part of my recovery journey.

During that work there were countless times when deeply buried memories surfaced and I would become utterly disconsolate, with gut wrenching soulful tears streaming from my eyes.

Reliving those events was utterly disgusting to me as an adult. At the time, I felt that death itself would have provided a welcome relief. Instead, I kept on keeping on, doing my best daily.

Early in my emotional-recovery process, I went to the local Walmart store in Palestine. My mission was to find a stuffed animal I could hold onto at night. A single man, I found that simply holding onto a pillow, as memories flooded in from being sexually assaulted as a child, provided no comfort or emotional support for me at all.

I found a soft, fluffy rabbit on sale and paid the store a whopping four dollars for it. Starting that night and for countless others, I held the rabbit in a death grip. I would cry myself to sleep with deep, soulful, bed-shaking sobs. How could grownups do what they did to me?

I wasn't in denial or mad at them. Instead, I was dealing with the incredible shame, embarrassment and guilt I had carried within, well into my senior years, despite the fact I knew what happened wasn't my fault.

Having a stuffed animal to hold onto at night meant the difference between wanting to awaken the next morning or not.

"Rabbit," as I named him, still sits on a shelf in my bedroom. He is a reminder of the power a stuffed animal has for a child, as well as for an adult recovering from memories of being sexually assaulted as a child.

My new friend was always there for me, just as my favorite stuffed teddy bear had been when I was a tyke. Rabbit listened, never shamed me, and never told me it was my fault. He never belittled me, ignored me or made me feel like I was a bother.

He always, always listened and cared in the best way he knew how. When I awakened each morning he was there, and I knew he loved me. After all, that's all I had wanted as a child, to love others and be loved in return.

Back then, my favorite teddy bear gave me the same gifts as Rabbit did when I was an adult. Plus, as a child, I knew that bear was mine and it's OK for a child to have a stuffed animal.

At least I received no shame for taking him to bed with me. I had endured what no child on planet Earth ever, ever should experience. To this day I'm deeply grateful for Rabbit and the teddy bears I had as a child.

Stuffed animals can have great power. Ask any child or adult recovering from being abused.

Stuffed animals have much more power than most adults realize. For a traumatized child, and even for a traumatized adult, they have healing powers even in their silence.

6

Affirmations

While I was working through hideous emotional wounds from childhood I was also on a different quest. Each time I entered a bookstore at least one book would virtually fall off the shelf into my hands.

Those books helped me find truths in my spiritual quest. Each helped open my eyes, heart and mind as to what for me is now real.

One that helped me the most was the late Louise Hay's book, *You Can Heal Your Life.*

It was the second edition of the book and I commend it to everyone. In that book she brought home to me the power of affirmations.

I had never read much about affirmations nor tried them before. This time however, I decided to do as she suggested. My life was such a wreck at that point that anything positive was desperately welcomed.

I was dealing with newly mined memories in all categories of abuse I experienced as a child. On top of that, I was going through a divorce. Back then, my feelings of self-worth were lower than the bottom of the deepest ocean.

One weekend I pondered coming up with two different affirmations. The first I wrote was "I'm growing younger as I age."

I use the affirmation:
"I'm growing younger as I age."
It has worked for me!

I hadn't hit fifty yet, but the aging process was something I didn't look forward to. Thanks to my dad I have a crease in my skull from when he had me kneel down at home one night. He put his right hand on the back of my head, and slammed the front of my head into the sharp edge of a door jamb. I had made it to age four by then.

By the time I was a teenager I saw the crease in my skull in the mirror and wanted no one else to see it - ever. Somehow, I just knew, even then.

My hope was that I would keep enough hair on the back of the crown of my head to hide a knot that was there, which I know is tied to my childhood. I don't have the video memory of what happened though. I've lost that battle and it has taken years for me to accept it, to bless and love it as a piece of me.

A couple of years after I started using my first affirmation, I suddenly had five clients at the Cartmell Home in Palestine, an extended-care facility, a first in my law practice.

Before then, I had a client whose mother-in-law and father-in-law had been residents of that facility. His name was Dr. Gordon McFarland.

Dr. McFarland was a gentleman and a genuinely good person. He was a hand surgeon who practiced at the famed Ochsner Hospital in New Orleans.

Of all the extended-care facilities he had been in, the Cartmell Home was the best-run and by far the cleanest, according to Dr. McFarland.

By the time I had those five clients I had learned that life is metaphorical. The reason they all contacted me about the same time was up to me to discern.

My "aha" moment came when I realized my affirmation could set me up for unintended consequences later in life, as I left the state of my being up to chance.

After a bit of thought, I improved it by adding, "...and I shall remain emotionally, mentally and physically healthy as I age."

I attribute that affirmation for my appearance being younger than my true age. Many people who don't know me believe I look younger than I am.

The second affirmation I wrote that day was, "Today is better than yesterday." That's a very simple statement, but was an important one for me back then.

My recovery process was arduous and insidiously painful. There were days when out-of-the-blue a stunning emotional wave, like an eight-foot saltwater breaker, would knock me down from behind. Each one sent me into heaving tears that were too many to count.

My emotional recovery was a steep, slippery slope with sharp, jagged rocks, crags and crevices. Yes, there were all sorts of painful falls on the way to the bottom, too. When I first started the recovery work, I couldn't see what was possible after lifting myself off the bottom.

No one could take the journey with me, but I was blessed to have a friend or two to encourage me. Their words of patience and encouragement were just enough to help me keep up my determination. I stuck with the process to overcome the emotional triggers of my past.

Looking back, after a year of practicing that affirmation, plus doing the work that Sara guided me to, I had made significant progress.

What I taught myself was that by reading, thinking, or writing the affirmation you add a drop of water to the jar you desire to be full. Every day I added a drop of water to my jar of inner peace. I did so by reading the affirmation and knowing it was true.

Affirmations can work. They are a powerful tool. Making them come true takes consistent effort on our part over time. Everything worthwhile does.

My today is better than my yesterday because I choose to make it be so.

7

Summer Camp

Though I was a young child, I remember when Tom Price came to Palestine. His wife, Leona, had contacted my mom, who put together a small group of my friend's moms to watch his short movie.

In those days, Tom was the camp director for a boys' summer camp named Rio Vista, located on the Guadalupe River, a few miles west of Kerrville in the Texas Hill Country.

Tom and his wife came to town, showed the video, and answered questions about the camp. At that point, I had never been told that going to summer camp was an option.

I remember the green metal trunk mom and dad bought for me. Jackie filled it with everything I needed for the month of June each year I went to camp. Summer camp was an enormous blessing in my life. I made friends from all over the state of Texas.

The first term at camp was a hard load for me, though. Many nights I silently cried myself to sleep, as I felt abandoned. Now, as an adult, I know that makes no sense.

Sam, from South Texas, was my Senior Counselor that year and took me under his wing. At night he let me know I was safe and protected. He also gave me words of encouragement that all the day's activities were just a few hours away.

My innermost fear then was that my mom and dad wouldn't come back to pick me up. As an adult, I know that is an absurd thought, but to my eight-year-old-self it was real. As you will read later in this book, I didn't have a clue about the severity of my abandonment issues until I was almost finished writing this book.

Every camper was assigned to a tribe. I was selected to be in the Golden Arrow tribe. An equal number of campers were in the rival Sioux tribe.

Each tribe had a tribal chief plus a brave for each age group. I served my tribe in each of the rest of my summer camp sessions as a brave and then as tribal chief the final year.

There was special recognition of certain campers who were selected based on character. They were the White Arrow campers. On Sunday nights the White Arrow chief and three of his braves paddled a canoe down the Guadalupe River, starting at the senior swimming dock and ending at the junior one.

Also in the canoe was the drummer, who slowly beat the drum as they paddled the two hundred yards or so. The White Arrows in the canoe had their faces painted and were shirtless, wearing loincloths as their only clothing, and one held a kerosene-soaked torch to light the way.

The chief came armed with wreaths woven from stems and leaves from the weeping willow trees that grew on the banks of the Guadalupe River.

The only other light during the ceremony came from torches the White Arrows had prepared at the edge of the swimming dock. Burlap sacks were wired to the tops of the cedar poles. The tops of those poles were soaked in kerosene for hours before they were lit for the Sunday night event.

The ceremony was solemn. Campers were required to be silent for its entirety. The White Arrow Chief who brought wreaths in the canoe placed one on the head of the selected campers each Sunday night. It was a high honor to be selected. I received a White Arrow award each summer camp session I attended.

Each morning there were two inspections. One was personal inspection and the other was cabin inspection. Those who won the personal inspection for their cabin were rewarded with an extra scoop of ice cream at lunch that day. That was a big deal for us campers!

The entire cabin of campers who won cabin inspection for the day received an extra scoop of ice cream as well. There were all sorts of activities for which you were graded to win tribal points. They ranged from canoeing to crafts, horseback riding to swimming. In each activity there was a counselor who was in charge, most of whom were college age.

Each counselor taught campers how to do the activity correctly and helped them improve their skills.

Of the many things my parents did for me, sending me to summer camp helped me in more ways than I would have thought of.

Summer camp gave me a break from the unhappy household I lived in. It also helped me break out of the shell of a child I kept myself in then.

I learned leadership skills, became more comfortable being myself, and became a much stronger swimmer. I also learned to be comfortable at night away from my growing-up home.

8

Out of Nowhere

On one or more late nights a month, I would be taken to a meeting by my dad. It was usually held in a secret room, or at the farm of one of the men in their group.

There were other men who came, most of them friends or acquaintances of my dad. Lighting at the farm was by car headlight and lanterns. The secret room was poorly ventilated and always had a musty smell. I remember there were metal chairs and an old sofa for sitting.

One of the leaders of the group was a man from out of town. I'll say his name was Sam. Sometimes I was given a special drink with something in it that was supposed to make me forget what I saw that evening.

My recollection is that the meetings were solemn occasions. In the group's quest to connect with the light (home or heaven, some would say) I saw things no child should ever witness.

It seems that gypsies were their favorite subjects. That's because there was no trail left before or behind them.

A table was set up as an altar. Even as a tyke, I sensed that what happened on those nights didn't seem to jibe with what was being taught in Sunday church services.

Later in life, I became determined to improve myself. This was a couple of years before those "blessed" muscle memories came back to pound on my head and shoulders.

As I began my quest as an adult to find my true self, I worked with a clairvoyant, Mary. That was before I met either Judy Goodman or Sara Hays.

Mary lived on the West Coast and we had several one-hour telephone sessions. In our second conversation she told me that she had seen some of my past. There were parts so completely blacked out that she couldn't see them, but she knew the memories were awful.

After another session or so she told me she was permitted to see my blacked-out memories and was horrified by what she saw. Mary told me it was so bad that she wouldn't tell me a thing about them.

Years later, on a sunny Saturday afternoon after I had mowed the yard and put the tools away, I had another surprise. The summer weather that afternoon was dead still. No dogs barking, no cars driving by, just silence.

I was on the upper tier of my backyard. Suddenly, I heard a "whoosh" coming from above.

"Kerplunk!"

Something hit the ground right beside me. I bent over to see what had fallen.

It was a chunk of bone.

I pay close attention to life's puzzle pieces.
There's always a message to be discerned.

I looked up at the majestic pine tree I was standing under. There wasn't a branch directly above me from which something solid could have fallen.

By then, I had recovered some memories of things that had happened in the room and at the farm. Most of the memories were faint.

The bone that fell beside me had a message I had to figure out. I tried and tried, but knew I had to keep the bone, and whatever message it had for me, to myself, or until the right person and time occurred.

With all the codependent traits I carried back then, I always felt guilty for anything bad happening, even if I wasn't to blame.

A few years ago, I talked to Renee Bouma, my dear friend and energy wellness business partner, about the piece of bone and the feelings it brought up for me. She tuned into her intuitive channels and gave me some profound information.

Renee informed me that the bone was sent by a man who had been badly harmed by the group of men. The man, now dead, wanted me to know he didn't hold what happened to him against me. At the time it happened, I was four.

The message Renee delivered from the man lifted a heavy burden I had carried for years.

The man forgave me readily and asked that I forgive myself, for he knew I was a tool for those mean men, the same as he was.

Although learning of his forgiveness lifted an enormous burden off my shoulders, I knew there were still other pieces I had to release.

9

It's Just an Iron Skillet

Post-divorce, I briefly dated a lady in the Dallas-Fort Worth area who was a talented cook. One evening Margie prepared a scrumptious meal. Chicken Cordon Bleu was the main course, a delicious choice.

After dinner I offered to wash the dishes for her. Margie preferred to hand wash them rather than put them in her dishwasher. Margie also preferred to handle the dishwashing chore herself, but she did ask me to dry the dishes.

I gladly complied. Little did I know that the iron skillet she had used to cook the main course had a profound message for me.

After Margie washed her treasured iron skillet she handed it to me to dry. I had a shocking experience when I grabbed its handle. I've dried iron skillets at home countless times, as a child, adolescent and adult. Each was dried without incident.

This time was quite different, as my right arm all but went limp. It seemed to want nothing to do with her iron skillet.

It took a near miracle for me to hold onto the skillet and keep it from crashing into my host's expensive glassware on her granite countertop.

I knew something was off kilter, but at the time I didn't know what or why.

Fast forward a year. I had traveled to Columbus, Georgia, for a session with Judy Goodman.

Judy helped me reach a hypnotic state, then took me back to the time when the back of my head was greeted by Jackie's (my mom) iron skillet. I was three years old.

With Judy's help, I saw my mind's video of that experience.

Only God knows what I had done, or not done, to set my mom off. Thank goodness Georgia, her maid, was there that morning.

Jackie swung the iron skillet like a tennis racquet, bashing the back of my head so hard I was knocked unconscious and fell face first to the floor.

While unconscious for a few minutes, I was taken out of my body. (That means that my soul, or spirit within me, was taken to the spiritual realm for a brief period of time.)

I was taken to the most beautiful garden I had ever seen in my life! The colors were more brilliant and intense than any I've seen on earth.

I was placed on Jeshua's (Jesus') knee. How incredibly gentle he was with me. (This brings deep soulful tears to my heart as I write about him.)

In the garden were beautiful flowers, amazing butterflies, singing birds and a sweet, loving, gentle lamb.

The lamb came up and nuzzled me in a nurturing way. Her fleece felt like the softest cashmere ever woven.

It was in that garden that I received spiritual and physical help for what had just happened to my little-boy body.

Faster than I wanted to return, I was sent back into my body. I had a pounding headache that chased me hard for the rest of the day, and it took days for the knot on my head to go away.

A few years later, I learned what lambs really smell and feel like. Oh, my goodness, their odor is pungent, and their fleece feels more like a wire brush than cashmere.

As my head became a frequent target for Jackie's rage, someone on the other side came through for me once again. I subconsciously learned how to transfer the pain in my head from being smacked by Jackie's 18" mahogany colored bat, down to my shoulders.

I don't suggest that as a healing technique for anyone else. For me, though, it was a survival tool.

To me, as an adult, an 18" bat looks harmless. As a three-year-old child, it was a weapon capable of delivering a death blow.

After Jackie died, I absolutely dreaded Mother's Day for years. Her mahogany bat blows to my head and shoulders were but one of the reasons I found it so hard to honor her memory on that annual day.

Sara's forgiveness exercise, which is detailed in a later chapter, helped me greatly.

"Dealing with our past memories (the known and forgotten) and our buried emotional pain is a prerequisite course for the empowering class of forgiveness."

Jackson Hanks

10

Panic From Shrimp Salad

After my divorce I was on a quest to find my perfect companion. Years down the road I look back at myself and shake my head in disbelief.

I've come a long way since then, gaining emotional maturity and wisdom. Now I know that to have the best companion relationship possible it's vital to first be best friends.

Within a couple of years, I met a nice lady via an online dating service. We had common professional careers and social interests. Nancy lived outside of a thriving town in Arkansas that was within driving distance for me.

We agreed to meet one weekend. She invited me to have a home-cooked meal as she preferred that over dining out. That would be a treat for me!

Nancy lived in a wonderful cabin in the woods, surrounded by nature on all sides. The menu for the night was a shrimp scampi salad with doctored-up black beans as a side dish. She asked me to be her helper in the kitchen. I was more than happy to do what I could.

We took our freshly prepared meal out to her back deck. It was a delightful evening, with temperatures in the 70s, a clear sky and very light breeze. Autumn was just around the corner.

Our conversation ranged from work matters to spiritual and metaphysical topics. She was a very interesting lady.

Nancy took one bite of her garlic-seasoned shrimp and things changed dramatically. The change was immediate, as she had an abreaction to what she put into her mouth. As I later learned from Sara, abreaction is when a person becomes consciously aware of repressed traumatic events.

After Nancy took that bite, her tone of voice changed, as did the conversation. I had never been exposed to, or trained how to deal with, a person who goes into a full-fledged panic attack. Out of necessity, I called on every skill I had, plus I used my intuition.

Memories can cause a panic attack.

For whatever reason, she said it was the texture of the shrimp that caused her to abreact. Then she went on a verbal rant that frightened me.

The shrimp took her back to times when she recalled being sexually assaulted by a male family member. Her memories were vivid. She was in a highly charged emotional state.

Intuitively, I knew the best thing to do was to listen. I did so as calmly as possible. Bit by bit I managed to get her to climb down the ladder of her highly charged state. I wasn't the problem, but to me the outcome was uncertain from the get-go.

It took several hours for Nancy to become emotionally calm. We then moved the conversation inside her cabin and cleaned the kitchen before retiring.

I slept on a downstairs couch that night, getting a few hours' sleep with "one eye open." When I heard her feet hit the floor upstairs, I went to check on her each time.

Finally, dawn came. All was OK with Nancy by then. I stayed in touch with her for a spell to make sure she was safe. Apparently, instead of dealing with her past, Nancy had buried herself in her businesses.

I hope and pray she did the work to overcome her insidious family past that caused the abreaction. In my case, ignoring my past, as I unwittingly did for years, only added to my opportunities for self-healing.

I am grateful I was able to help Nancy calm down enough to hear her own voice of sense and reason that night. It was a frightening and brand-new experience for me.

11

Lessons Learned From Death

Death is inevitable. We all know that.

In each of our families the reasons and order in which deaths occur vary widely. Family members dying came with frequency from an early age for me.

My paternal grandfather, Clyde Hanks, started the parade in 1956 when I was four, dying of a heart attack. Lula Rayburn, my maternal grandmother, died in 1958. She too died of a heart attack. Then Clyde's wife, Zula Hanks, died of a heart attack in 1960.

I was twelve when my father died unexpectedly at age forty-seven in 1964. His listed cause of death was a heart attack.

The day my dad died is one I'll always vividly remember. I was in the seventh grade, and it started off as a normal school day. At lunch time I was watching eighth graders play basketball in the gym, when a teacher found me and told me my mom was waiting for me outside. I was clueless as to why.

My mom and my sister were in the Ford family station wagon driven by one of our family friends, Wayne Smith, who died years later. It was a warm, sunny, windy day in December.

On any other day it would have been a great day to play outside after school. My mom and sister were sobbing. Mr. Smith told me that my dad was dead.

On the day of Jack's funeral, two days after he died, a blue norther, as we call them in Texas, had blown in. It was cloudy and cold enough to snow. Words read at his funeral were ones I wrapped myself in for years. From John's gospel, those words were: "In my house are many mansions..."

Following Dad's death, our house was filled with company for a couple of weeks. His death was a shock to all who knew him, including his cardiologist in Houston, Dr. Lester Hoaglin.

Mom circled the wagons with my sister and me. The family dynamics changed in many ways. It was only after all the company stopped coming to visit that we could deal with our raw feelings.

As I later read books by Elizabeth Kubler-Ross, I realized another miracle had happened in my life. Somehow, I had managed to work through the five common steps of grief following the death of my dad. It took me a couple of years though.

The steps are: Shock/Denial, Anger, Bargaining, Depression and finally Acceptance. Those were the post-death emotional categories I worked through. From then until she died, my mom never made it past Anger.

Many years later my beloved second cousin, Susanna Garrison, died in 2001, at the age of ninety-one. My wife and I loved her dearly and named our first child after her.

Susanna's health had declined rapidly that year. Even so, her death was incredibly difficult for me. For many years she had been my anchor.

Susanna Garrison also provided a safe, fun place for our children to visit growing up, and they adored her.

I was utterly disconsolate at her funeral, choking back sobbing tears. I didn't want to be seen losing it in public. I lost it, however, when the hymn "On Eagles' Wings" was played and sung.

Susanna the elder, as I called her, had traits my mom severely lacked: warmth, kindness, wisdom and a genuine loving heart. She was kind to our children and loved them dearly.

Her death happened after I was divorced. I'll always remember the wonderful lady I was dating at the time, Carmen, calling me from Oklahoma the afternoon I learned of Susanna's death.

I was so utterly disconsolate on the phone that I could barely hear her words. I do remember the wonderful wisdom she gave me though.

"Jackson, just breathe," she said to me over and over again with great patience. By the end of our chat, I was in at least a functional emotional state.

As she taught me, tears release toxins. Plus, deep tears help release the incredibly deep feelings of loss I had just experienced.

With Susanna's death, I had lost a life navigator. Susanna was an accomplished woman. She helped lead the fight for Title IX in the NCAA while she was the head of women's athletics at the University of Houston.

Friends who honored Susanna at her retirement luncheon had memorialized her with a brick inscribed "Old Granite Head." She wasn't controlling, but a family trait we shared was being mightily determined!

Susanna never let honors of any kind affect her. Although my wife and I were close to her, we had to learn from the newspaper that she had been honored by the University of Houston. She was the head of women's athletics there for many years and later had a gymnasium named for her.

As Susanna would say, doing the right thing is far more important than being recognized for doing so.

Following my dad's death, determination was my guiding star. I set out to be as good as others thought my dad and his dad were.

I remember as a sophomore in high school I came across a poem written by Robert W. Service.

Part of the poem is copied below. The poem is entitled "The Quitter" and is in the public domain.

I didn't read Mr. Service's book in which the poem appeared. Yet I knew in my heart of hearts that emotional survival requires the kind of gritty determination he wrote about.

Death is a powerful teacher.

Death is a powerful, powerful teacher. I trust I have learned the lessons it came to teach me.

The Quitter
It's the plugging away that will win you the day,
So don't be a piker, old pard!
Just draw on your grit, it's so easy to quit.
It's the keeping-your-chin-up that's hard.
It's easy to cry that you're beaten - and die;
It's easy to crawfish and crawl
But to fight and to fight when hope's out of sight -
Why that's the best game of them all!
And though you come out of each grueling bout,
All broken and battered and scarred,
Just have one more try - it's so easy to die,
It's the keeping-on-living that's hard.

12

Ms. Harris

By the time I reached the second grade I was a bigger mess than my parents or I had any idea of. Fairly early in our work, my therapist, Sara, told me to get a copy of all my school pictures and look for distinct changes.

I did as suggested, and found a marked difference in my body language between my first and second grade pictures. My second-grade teacher, Ms. Harris, must have picked up on some things my pictures showed.

Nearly all my school friends were in Ms. Hearne's second-grade class, just down the hall. I made a few new friends in Ms. Harris' class, but there were no classmates who lived near me.

In first-grade my teacher, Ms. Scott, had wanted me to write with my right hand. I tried and the results weren't good, as I am a natural left-handed writer.

My mom was very displeased with my report cards, which always had a D in handwriting. Granted my penmanship wasn't up to what Ms. Scott wanted from me, but I always did the best I knew how to.

Ms. Harris knew I was behind in penmanship but also saw me falling behind in spelling. What she was teaching wasn't working for me.

I was falling behind in the second grade.

She and my parents had me do remedial work with handwriting and with phonics workbooks every school day. That went on for months.

Though it was hard at the time, my parents required school work to be finished before engaging in playtime, whether inside or outside. Now I had regular homework plus remedial homework. It was difficult, because I was slow to catch on.

In time the remedial work paid off handsomely, as I became an excellent speller by the time I reached the fourth grade. That gift carries forward to this day. I am grateful too that I learned the importance of doing homework before playtime as a child.

Ms. Harris blessed me and the rest of our class with another gift too, one I will always appreciate. She gave us worksheets with pictures of local songbirds to color.

We learned about their habitats and songs. Then she asked us to come back to class and tell what we had seen and heard the day before.

Though I already loved birds, this exercise helped boost my self-confidence and self-esteem. By then, I already recognized mockingbirds, cardinals, blue jays, hummingbirds, crows, wood thrashers, wood thrushes, yellow-bellied flickers and house wrens.

That year I learned to recognize black-capped chickadees, titmice, scissor-tailed flycatchers and cedar waxwings as well. I felt good each time I learned about and recognized a new species.

Ms. Harris had no idea of what had happened in my life before I became her student. I remain deeply grateful to her for her teachings, her patience with me, and just for caring about a child who desperately needed help. She was the encouraging teacher I had never had before.

I had no idea at the time how crucial second grade was for me. Thanks to Ms. Harris' encouragement, I was able to get back on track with my school work.

Even more importantly, I overcame my dreaded angst about school days - my constant fear that someone would see in my eyes and/or body what had happened to me at home and other places.

As a bonus, Ms. Harris helped me find a safety zone. I was safe and out of danger when watching and learning about birds in my backyard.

13

Life is Metaphorical

In the early 1990s a community row was going on. I was the mayor of Palestine, Texas at the time.

The town had a for-profit hospital, Trinity Valley Medical Center, which was fighting tooth and toenail against the county-owned non-profit hospital, Memorial Hospital.

Memorial Hospital had an outdated facility. They sought to build a new hospital, but needed to issue bonds to finance it.

It seemed everyone in town had an opinion. All the town's doctors practiced at one of the hospitals, but not at both.

As mayor I wanted both hospitals to succeed. Memorial Hospital threatened to shut down if they were not able to build a new facility. I considered it to be a very real possibility. The prospect of losing a few hundred jobs in our community made my decision a very easy one, even though the city was asked to allow the county owned non-profit entity to use the city's credit rating to help it secure financing.

On a close vote the council agreed to allow its credit rating to be used by Memorial Hospital, granting it a new lease on life. It opened in a beautiful new building a couple of years later and hired more employees for its workforce.

Being mayor and working with the council provided me an avenue for being of service. Holding such an office also meant that, as with my law practice but even more so, my public standing and people's perception of my character, was important.

In those days, Palestine had an annual Cattle Baron's Ball benefitting the American Cancer Society. Statistically, our county raised more money per capita for the American Cancer Society than any other county in Texas.

All thanks to the heroic efforts of the Ball's chairwomen. Saying "no" to them was not an option!

The Cattle Baron's Ball was held at the Anderson County Youth Livestock Arena and grounds on the second Saturday evening/night in August. Even though it was hot, people always turned out for the Ball in droves.

My wife and I bought tickets and planned to go as a couple, until she received a call mid-afternoon. Our evening's babysitter had cancelled on us.

Since I was (and still am) an early morning person, we decided that I'd go to the Ball for the first hour and a half and return home. I did, just as we agreed. My wife then went to the ball to socialize with her friends and stayed until about midnight. I had no inkling of what was about to happen.

The following Monday afternoon I received a call from a lawyer friend of mine. He let me know that John McDonald, a well-known local lawyer, had told him that the city police had been called out to a local residence on the night of the Cattle Baron's Ball and that I had been found in bed with a local woman's husband.

I thanked my fellow lawyer for letting me know what he had heard. There was not an inkling of truth to it whatsoever.

I had gone straight home from the ball at the appointed time and taken up kiddo-watching duty. That night the Dallas Cowboys played their annual pre-season football game against the Houston Oilers.

Two of our three girls were out on sleep-overs. Once the youngest was in bed I watched a bit of the game, and then called it a night.

John McDonald was well known for his personality. Bragging came as naturally to him as water flowing downhill. It seems he was spreading a vicious false rumor about me for no good reason.

Back then, I was not consciously aware in any way. I had no idea how to energetically handle the situation I was facing.

I live in a small town in rural East Texas. In our community there are plenty of good folks, but there are also plenty of folks who enjoy spreading gossip.

Certain ones like it even better when something bad happens to others.

I had spent my entire professional career doing all I could to build my reputation in town so that I would attract the right type of clients for my law practice. From the start, I innately knew the importance of giving back to community and did so with gusto.

I served on many non-profit boards and committees. A few of them I helped get off the ground by donating both my time and legal services.

The rumor soon spread. Our young girls heard the accusations from some of their friends in elementary school. My wife received calls at home, hearing the same garbage.

Since the city police had allegedly been called out to the scene, I asked the city manager to get in touch with the police chief. I asked that the police tapes be run for that night. They did, and of course no such call was received by the police department.

My employees told me they had people come up to them in grocery stores saying they would never use my services again. I was utterly crushed when they told me that bit of information.

By Tuesday morning the rumor of my whereabouts and doings on the night of the ball had spread like wildfire. I had no idea that a life lesson had just amped up its game and smacked me with a gut-wrenching sucker punch.

It was so tough that we hired a private investigator, and then a lawyer in Tyler, to pursue damages for slander. As a public official in Texas, to win a slander lawsuit you not only have to prove you were slandered and suffered damage, you also have to prove intent to harm.

Years later, I learned from my good friend and extraordinarily gifted clairvoyant, Judy Goodman, that we come in with three or possibly four life-lessons to learn. She taught me that if we miss learning them, the lesson will be repeated over and over until it's learned.

Since then, I've taught myself that unlearned lessons change faces, places and time, but increase with intensity each time they are missed. It seems I didn't figure out that the lesson of "invalidation" had been chasing me for most of my life.

For example, in high school, two of us were nominated for Most Representative Boy. The other candidate played football and was well liked. I wasn't a jock, but served by helping out with the high school's yearbook. I was in charge of its advertising campaign.

My sister had been voted Arc Light Sweetheart her junior and senior years. Jackie really wanted me to receive the award. Looking back, it's easy to see why as the recipient received a large painting of themselves.

Shortly before the vote was taken, I was told by one of my female friends that my opponent was actively campaigning to win the vote. I was beyond shocked. To my knowledge, no one had ever campaigned to receive the Most Representative Boy Student Award.

I never asked anyone to vote for me, as I didn't believe that was becoming of the school's most representative boy.

You already know the outcome. My opponent won handily. I was bummed out, but congratulated him on winning.

The obvious in life isn't what's most important. It's the unseen metaphors that life throws in our path.

A little more than two years after being slandered, invalidation paid me another visit. I was in Washington State being the driver/porter for Uncle Clyde and Aunt Howard as they vacationed at the Resort at Port Ludlow.

The lawyer we had hired to file the slander suit let us know that he had allowed the statute of limitations to lapse before filing the suit. By that time, my emotional capital spent trying to recoup what had been lost had run out.

My wife and I could have filed a different suit against the lawyer who had made a serious professional mistake. Instead, we chose to let it go, doing our best to get an apology from John McDonald. A veiled one came out in the newspaper when the hearing to dismiss our suit (filed too late) was heard.

Years later, I invited "Invalidation" to come stand beside me so I could have a chat with it. With clarity I let it know that I had learned its lesson well and that its presence in my life was no longer necessary.

With energetic truth in the words I spoke, the lesson of invalidation disappeared. It made one more little attempt in 2013, but I caught it quickly and had a second chat with it.

The response and result were the same. I've learned the lesson invalidation teaches.

Life is metaphorical!

Life is metaphorical. Our lessons have to be dug out of the invisible realm within us.

Invalidation was a powerful lesson for me. After the fact, I learned about the power life lessons have.

14

Messages in Water

My codependent traits are tapes that were instilled in childhood. It's taken countless books, hours in therapy with Sara, and help from my dear friends, Judy Goodman and Renee Bouma, to reach the emotionally healthy place where I am today.

It is a good place, but as a survivor, I must always be on the lookout for the next emotional pothole in my life. I also take positive steps to keep myself in the best place possible.

In 2003, Sara instructed me to attend Al-Anon classes, where I learned several valuable bits of wisdom. One of those was the importance of being grateful. It sounds too simple to be that powerful, yet I've learned it truly is.

Dr. Masaru Emoto was an esteemed Japanese physicist. His book, *The Hidden Messages in Water*, is on my list of the top five books I've ever read. I had previously read his book *Messages in Water,* featuring numerous pictures of water crystals.

Through his micron microscope, Dr. Emoto (who died in 2014) scientifically proved that water crystals are impacted by human thoughts, words and music.

Growing up, I was taught that the human body is seventy percent water. Now science is teaching that our bodies are ninety percent water.

In *The Hidden Messages in Water* (2004), Dr. Emoto asked a question of his readers - what are the two most powerful human emotions? My immediate thought went to love and fear, as to me they are the mothers of all other human emotions.

When I read what Dr. Emoto said were the two most powerful human emotions to him, I laughed out loud. It was a tremendous reminder for me. I had forgotten that important piece of wisdom learned from Al-Anon.

Love and gratitude are life's most powerful emotions.

Previously, I learned from Sara that love is a powerful emotion. Yet she also said that human love always has an agenda.

Before I did the child within work with Sara, I took an Access Consciousness class from its creator and teacher, Gary Douglas. In that class I learned something that I have practiced countless times. I used it frequently in my emotional recovery work.

That pearl of wisdom is this:

"How does it get any better than this?"

As he taught, and I practiced, "How does it get any better than this?" became a real question, not a statement.

When used as a statement or sentence, I feel the energy of it and it's as flat as a pancake. When used as a question, the energy flows strongly because of Universal principles. When you ask, "How does it get any better than this?" it puts you in a state of gratitude. On planet Earth there always is, and always will be, someone in more dire straits than you.

Dr. Emoto's books show pictures of how our music impacts water crystals. The difference between their appearances from being exposed to music composed by Mozart versus current grunge music was profound.

Prayers are impactful, too, according to Dr. Emoto's research. He showed what water crystals from an environmentally sick lake in Brazil looked like, both before and after healing prayers were said for it.

The polluted lake's water crystal pictures before receiving prayers were depressing to see, while the water crystals depicted after receiving healing prayers showed a remarkably positive change.

Dr. Emoto's words and pictures hammered home to me an important lesson - to be grateful for whatever it is I have and am going through. Being in gratitude puts me in a state of awareness, too.

Thank you with all my heart, Dr. Emoto, for your profound work. What an incredible wake-up call you gave me.

Seeing the physical response human thoughts, words and music have on water crystals profoundly impacted my life.

I do my best to be and bring blessings, encouragement and empowerment to others who come into my life.

Now, I seek to find the good in every person I come across, as well as to mine the good in whatever experiences I have.

15

Good Fences

The famous American humorist, Will Rogers, was quoted as saying, "Good fences make good neighbors." He was talking about ranchers' fences and cows.

In my journey, I have learned that my personal boundary fence and aura, or energetic fence, are just as important to me as good fences are to cattle ranchers. From Amorah Quan Yin in her book entitled *The Pleiadian Workbook* (1999), I learned that our aura (energy surrounding our body) normally extends outward, upward and downward two and a half to three feet.

That said, we are in charge of our personal energy. As suggested by Amorah Quan Yin, I experimented by shrinking my energy field to within a foot (never more!) and allowing it to expand without boundaries.

When I pulled my energy field close within (which is a good thing to do when you are in a crowd, I've learned) I felt condensed pressure near my body. It was a very uncomfortable feeling.

In nature, I allowed it to expand freely, as I was in a safe place. With no other humans nearby, it danced and played as a young child would.

Learning to shift my energy was step one in setting safe, protective and effective personal energetic boundaries. In my life, my energy field has been attacked more times than I can count.

I have experienced attacks from those who intend them, as well as those whose attacks came from their sub-conscious mind.

From 2001 through 2003 I did my best to heal from the new memories of what happened to me in childhood. At the same time, I was rapidly expanding my knowledge in new categories of books.

One Friday evening, I attended a social event for a short while. I came home and as was my habit at the time, sat down to write three prayers. That was a deep healing technique for me.

I managed to write two of them. Suddenly, my personal energy level dropped so low I couldn't keep my eyes open anymore and went to bed.

The next morning it felt as if someone had slipped a Mickey in the water I drank at the social event. My body felt healthy, but I barely had enough energy to take a forward step. As weak as I was, my Saturday list of things to do seemed formidable.

With my energy level so low, all I could do was to sit, which turned out to be a blessing in disguise.

I began to explore the energy fields that surrounded my body. Finally, I found a hole or tear in my outer energy field - where someone had attacked it and won the battle. Once they penetrated my field, they installed a siphon and were living off my energy instead of their own.

With that discovery, I removed the siphon by using my mind. I then sealed up my energy field as best I knew how at the time. Within seconds, my personal energy level increased to near normal levels. I never determined exactly who did the deed, though I have an idea. That part matters not. The attacking person likely could not live with just their own energy level. He/she found a subject who didn't adequately protect his energy field - me.

Whenever I go into a restaurant, a mall, or am around a crowd of people, I pull my energetic fence in to within a foot-and-a-half of my body. Then, when it's safe once again, I allow it to resume its normal distance.

In addition, I learned in the same book how to set energetic protections, besides setting energetic fences for myself. Amorah Quan Yin's suggestion to her readers was to do a couple of simple things.

First, surround your energetic fence with six inches of white light.

I practiced that time and time again, and did so to protect myself daily. This type of self-protection was not taught in law school!

At first, the white-light protections need to be refreshed during the day. With daily practice, I learned that energy follows thought. Then I set the protections for the time length I desire and they stay put.

As a second layer, Amorah Quan Yin suggested using violet as the base color for protection and to use two inches of it. Learning what worked best for me took much experimentation.

It's helpful to work with someone, as I was privileged to do with Judy Goodman, who sees or senses energy, its colors, vibrations and intensity.

Putting the violet layer on top of the white-light protection became my impenetrable protection, or so I thought. It worked at the beginning levels at least.

As with anything, as you become better at it there's always something new to learn. For my self-protection, I continue to learn to this day!

When I was a first-term mayor of our town in 1989, there was a city councilman who found fault with everything and everyone. Had Santa Claus shown up at a city council meeting, he would have berated him for not having a city permit.

Joe Ed Bunton had spent sixteen years in the United States Army, with the last three being in the Inspector General's Corps. To say he was an unhappy person is an extraordinary understatement.

Joe Ed would literally come within inches of your face to make his point. Back then, I had no idea how to set self-protections to prevent his outer self (aura) from touching and penetrating mine. It always felt like he'd jumped into my personal bucket of life - without an invitation! I always backed away from him and felt I had been violated.

Protect yourself with strong boundaries and energetic fences.

I am who I am today partially because I have learned the importance of energetic fences and how to effectively set personal protections. They create a safe zone for me.

Protections are important for me. Doing so allows me to spend my time in self-improvement. It also allows me to help others. My time is better spent that way instead of finding holes in my fences and rebuilding my energy levels.

16

More Tears

My family tree was small from the time I was born. My ex-wife's family tree is very large. So much so that a friend of hers once mused that if my ex-wife was the first human being to land on Mars she'd be greeted by cousins.

By the time I graduated from college I had very few living adult relatives. They consisted of a second cousin (Susanna Garrison), Uncle Clyde (my dad's brother) and my mom. All four grandparents, great aunts (two) and uncles (two) were deceased, as was my dad.

At an early age, I already had lots of practice in dealing with the loss of a family member. For some reason, I seemed to be the one who traveled with my mom to pack up and clean out her relatives' homes.

My mom was an only child, so I have learned some of the traits of only children, and do my best never to act like Jackie did.

I remember the last Thanksgiving dinner at my mom's house. My daughters came down for the Thanksgiving feast from Bedford, Texas, where they lived with their mom. My mom wasn't as strong as she used to be, so I volunteered to cook the Thanksgiving meal at my home and take it to her house.

My mother complained about the way I carved the turkey. After the meal she also let me know that I wasn't drying the dishes properly. Mind you, by this time I had carved her turkeys for almost forty years and dried dishes for longer.

After my dad's death, Jackie would always invite her friends, Ed and Katherine Herrington, to be her guests for holiday meals. Ed and Katherine were family friends who had no children. After they died, she began including Father Clay Piatt and his wife Suzie, until Father Clay's untimely death. Then it was Father Edward Blankenship. Everyone called him Father B.

Then Father Mike was invited along with Father B, as the latter had retired. They were the priests at St. Phillip's Episcopal Church in Palestine, Texas.

It was always a relief to have company during those celebratory meals. Jackie had to be on her best behavior, as she wanted to be seen as the person she wasn't when they weren't around.

Her meals were delicious, well-timed and featured excellent presentation. Holiday meals and entertaining were important to Jackie. She always did them well.

I always will remember when Susanna, our oldest daughter, was age five and Frances was age three. That year I made certain we had a memorable Thanksgiving meal at Grandma Jackie's.

In those days, Jackie smoked her own turkey. To add some humor to the event, I worked with Susanna for a couple of weeks so she could recite something after the Thanksgiving meal was over. I had her practice thanking Grandma Jackie for the delicious meal, but most especially for the smoked buzzard (turkey vulture) before we left the table. By Thanksgiving Day, she had it down pat.

It was mid-afternoon when everyone finished their dessert. Jackie's guests were about to leave so I looked at Susanna and under my breath reminded her of her manners.

Susanna then said, "Thank you, Grandma Jackie, for the wonderful meal and the delicious smoked buzzard."

Everyone belly laughed, but those words sent Grandma Jackie through the roof. I made sure Susanna was safe and later told my mom that I had put her up to it. Jackie's sense of humor was none too keen.

The next summer, Frances was at Jackie's by herself. She came home in tears and told her mom that Grandma Jackie had purposefully smashed the top of a music box on her tiny fingers.

My wife and I agreed that from that day forward no child of ours would ever be alone with Grandma Jackie. Our girls were blessed that their late maternal grandmother, Lucille Reeves, was Jackie's polar opposite.

All of Lucille's many grandchildren adored and loved her, as she was the grandmother every grandchild would want to have!

Many years after my dad died, I learned that I had been "spousified" by Jackie. My duties went far beyond that of being a teenage son. I had no idea the impact that would have on me as an adult.

After my dad died on December 15th, 1964, my sister and I pooled our meager resources to buy Jackie a couple of Christmas gifts. My sister found a pretty dress at the Jay Shop for our mom's Christmas, along with some new perfume.

Jackie liked our gifts so well that she returned both for something else. I was heartbroken, and bet my sister was, too. Our best just wasn't good enough for the woman.

By the time Jackie was an octogenarian, she began having serious health problems. There were numerous times I'd receive a call from her in the middle of the night.

Jackie would ask me to take her to the local emergency room, which I dutifully did. Then I stayed in the room with her until the attending physician released her.

I never thought much of it until I worked with Sara. Though Jackie was in her eighties, physically feeble, and prone on the emergency room bed, I always made certain to stay at least a full arm's length from her.

Subconsciously, I guess, I remembered the iron skillet treatment from age three.

In her mid-eighties, she no longer could do everything for herself. My sister and I helped move her into Sterling House, a local assisted-living facility.

She stayed there for a few years. Then one afternoon she fell in the bathroom and ended up with a broken leg. I wondered whether her brittle bone broke, thus causing her fall.

After surgery she was in ICU for a few days, where I went to visit her one morning. Jackie's eyes were closed but she was having a conversation with someone.

The language Jackie was using was one I had never heard before. I couldn't make out a single word she said.

Soon thereafter, Jackie returned to Sterling House where her feeble body gave out. She died very early in the morning a few weeks later.

During the next month, whenever I received a condolence or something as simple as a two-second human hug, I absolutely melted into deep tears. By the end of that month, I knew something was way off kilter with me.

By that time in my life I had had lots of practice in dealing with the death of loved ones. My reaction was quite different this time, though.

Two weeks later I was in Sara's office. I knew I needed her psychological help.

I let her know that mom had died and how each act of human kindness given to me thereafter impacted me emotionally. Each time I melted, sobbing.

Sara looked at me and said, "Jackson, what's wrong with that?" It took me what seemed like forever, but likely was only about fifteen seconds, when I managed this reply, "Absolutely nothing."

I have no idea where those words came from, as I was still programmed that everything was my fault.

Then Sara gave me this bit of amazing wisdom.

"Jackson, you are not grieving the loss of your mother. You are grieving for the mother you never had."

Sara was spot on. Thanks to my childhood, I grieved for the mother I never had.

With that I shed more tears, but I knew why. Sara had spoken the truth.

I'm very grateful to my mom for all the good things she did for me while she was alive. And until I die, I will always be working to lessen the impact of the emotional trash and physical wounds I bear because of her.

Sara's wisdom helped me turn a sharp emotional corner in my life, once again.

17

Gypsy Dawn

During the fall of 2017 I became determined to remember a horrific event from my childhood. I had only vague memories until I went into a meditative state.

That is when I reached out and was able to contact a lady who told me her name was Gypsy Dawn. What follows in italics were her words.

"Unbathed and usually hungry, we travel in bands. Sometimes we have to steal to get money to buy the necessities of life: food, something to wear, water, and from time to time, a place to stay.

Our bands are like Indian tribes. Each one is different, but all have a leader.

From time to time a member breaks off and tries to make a go of it on his or her own. We discourage that, as a lone wolf lacks the protection of its pack.

Each of our members has a skill set. That's so we can get day jobs, which in the mid fifties was much easier for men than women.

As we enter towns, we spread out on foot. Some will ride in the only car we have among us, which is a nearly always a worn-out jalopy.

There are towns that give us little trouble and those that give us a lot. We try to avoid the latter ones.

My name is Gypsy Dawn. I had never been to Palestine, Texas, before. It seemed to be a quaint town, just like others we travel through in East Texas.

I didn't know a soul in town except the troupe I traveled with. I was walking, and a friendly man offered me a ride and asked if I needed a place to stay.

Little did I know what his intentions were. Not just his, but those of his friends, too.

He bought a sandwich for me for my supper. It was my last meal, though I didn't realize that at the time.

I was told that after a night meeting he'd put me up in a motel for the rest of the night. That would have beaten sleeping in the car for another night.

We went somewhere out in the country. There was a strange odor in the air, one I had never smelled before, and I was given something to drink which made me feel good.

A sort of altar had been set up. Close to it was a table that had a wooden box draped with red cloth. I was told it was a ceremonial table and that I was to be its honored guest that night.

I was told that I would be given medicine and would only feel a pin prick when blood was drawn to determine its type.

Knowing I was outnumbered and wasn't body-building strong anyway, I went along, thinking that I'd get through the night somehow. I did, but ended up in a place I didn't fathom possible.

As things really got cranked up, there were adults and a kid watching, my head started spinning and I became a bit woozy.

Then as matters progressed, a stool was brought so that a youngster could reach up and speak to me. He seemed genuinely kind and nice.

Soon, his adult leader brought out one of their ritual tools. It was a short saber knife. With a man's hand wrapped over the little boy's hand, the knife was plunged into my gut.

I came to strongly enough to verbally attack the grown men with all I had left in me. I knew I was bleeding, but thought the wounds were minor.

The man poured something on the wounds and gave me another cocktail to drink. The pain was excruciating. Whatever was in the cocktail eased the pain and made me feel happy again, almost unaware as the knife was plunged into my abdomen again and again.

Many, many years later, a nice, wise lady who is a good friend of the adult self of the little boy at the meeting reached out to, and found, my higher self (soul). I was glad to be contacted by her.

For me to move forward in my higher self's progression, I knew it was important that I respond to Renee Bouma. She came asking for forgiveness for the actions of the three-year-old boy back then.

It seems the little boy grew up, and as an adult recently began remembering some of the stuff that occurred in his childhood. A piece of bone was sent from the ethers to fall at his feet in his backyard one summer afternoon.

That started the process of the adult part of the little boy to get in touch with me. His childhood must have been extremely difficult. I saw the utter horror and remorse in his eyes when the adult pushed his hand, holding the knife, down into my gut.

I let the wise lady know that what happened that night was not the fault of the child. He was innocent and used as a wicked tool by the men who were there in the name of "the light."

They were guilty. He was not.

In my opinion, their experiments had nothing to do with 'the light.' Rather they were rituals from the dark realms, masked and disguised in the name of 'the light.'

Gypsies always are hard to trace. Back then, they were expendable, too.

If I could have taken that little boy's pain with me, I would have. In my heart of hearts, I knew he had no idea what the consequences would be of what he had been forced to do.

I'm so sorry it deeply impacted him for the length of time it did. I am glad he received my forgiveness with grace and love. It wasn't his fault at all.

He was the victim of ritual abuse, just as I was."

Gypsy Dawn

Even though I've seen myself in several past lives, I've feared dying for many years, but had no idea why.

During a powerful session during the fall of 2017 with Frankie Burget, the myofascial therapist, I learned that I carried a mark and energy of what I did as a three-year-old. Frankie's myofascial touch is amazing.

As you will learn in another chapter, I first released abandonment issues that have been with me since childhood in that session. Then, like rungs on a ladder, Frankie went to the next location she saw needed help, in my stomach area.

She asked what feeling was there. I told her it was sadness, which cleared out of the way quickly. Then she went to the last rung on the ladder, so to speak. She told me that I didn't have to say the word, but for me to think it.

The word that came to my mind was gore. As she pressed slightly on an area in my lower left abdomen, my body kicked into high gear.

Tears came streaming. My body flailed in all sorts of ways. I pounded my fists as my body shook violently. This lasted for several minutes.

Then all of a sudden, my body stopped. I felt enormously lighter, both emotionally and physically.

I sat up and told Frankie about Gypsy Dawn's story my three-year-old mind and body had held onto. She said she had seen the piece of energy I just released from my abdomen for years in our sessions, though my body hadn't been ready to release it until that morning.

As soon as the energy of that event was cleared from my inner child, I instantly lost my fear of dying.

Subconsciously, I had feared the consequences of carrying the energy of Gypsy Dawn's death across the veil when I die.

Ritual abuse is sometimes conducted in the name of "the light." I believe it is carried out in the name of darkness, regardless of what other name people claim to operate under. People get sucked in and are scarred for life and beyond.

Ritual abuse is insidious - and a haven for those in the dark realms.

Even those who watch in innocence, or are forced to participate, are given a sack load of stuff to carry that deeply impacts their lives. I know so, because I am one of them.

The burden was horrific, as I had been smudged by darkness.

18

Retrieving a Lost Piece
of My Childhood Self

My recovery journey has been an interesting one, to say the least. Several years after doing the child within work with Sara, I knew I was missing something important.

Pieces of my energetic body were stolen from me in childhood, as was my childhood innocence. I knew so because regardless of what I did, I never felt like my whole self.

In time, I talked to Judy Goodman. I learned from her about the seven realms of darkness and how they work.

She also taught me about the importance of having massive energetic protections with you should you enter even Level 1 (the entrance level) of those realms.

This included not just self-protections, but taking Archangel Michael with you as well as Jeshua (Jesus). Spiraling down into the energy and torment of souls is not for the faint of heart. It is wise to super protect yourself.

Even with the knowledge and tools I had on board back then, I had my concerns. When I knew the time was right for me, I also called in Quan Yin and my dear friend, Bruno Groening.

Bruno, not known by many in this country, was a carpenter in the mid to late 1940s who lived in Germany and would travel from town to town.

His healing gifts were extraordinary, and he'd draw throngs of people seeking help. Bruno gladly obliged but never charged a penny for his work. He truly had a heart of gold and would help anyone who asked. Bruno asked for nothing in return, as I learned through the years.

He told people that his gifts came from God and God doesn't charge him for them.

I know that when Bruno died, he decided not to go all the way back to his soul. In heaven (or home, as I call it) the soul lacks the ability to feel the emotional and physical pain we do on planet Earth. Bruno decided to stay in the astral plane instead. There he feels just what we feel, but has higher wisdom and guidance to help us.

One of the sexual/ritual abuse perpetrators had somehow found a way to keep a part of me to himself. I was three or four and hadn't a clue what I had lost when it happened. I felt different, lacking something invisible, but didn't even know how to verbalize my loss.

With help from Jeshua and others, I retrieved that missing piece of my soul by returning in my mind to that horrible night.

The sights, smell, oppressiveness, horrific energy and morbid screams I heard let me know I was in a place I wanted to leave as fast as possible.

Jeshua walked beside me as did Bruno, Quan Yin and Archangel Michael. I told the man who had placed my hand on the knife that I was here to recover the lost part he had stolen from me.

Given the company I was in, he immediately handed it over to me. Before I assimilated it back into my being, I asked that it be cleansed of all negative aspects I knew it had picked up from being in Hades for so long.

Once cleaned as best I knew how, with help from Jeshua, Quan Yin, Archangel Michael, and Bruno, I pulled the lost piece of me into its rightful place.

Doing so brought inner peace to my adult self. It also brought joy to my child within.

The dark realms are not to be messed with, though many do. Their residents have tricks up their sleeves to capture the innocent. They care not for the consequences, only the rewards they seek, as you have learned.

Those in darkness are always looking for their next meal. They get it by enticing others to join them in their evil endeavors.

19

Robbing the Giver
of Their Grace

When I first started writing prayers for healing in 2001 I would send them to Carmen, whom I was dating at the time. She had a master's degree in English and would point out my grammatical errors.

She also made editor's notes, so I could improve what I had written. More importantly though, she encouraged me to write them every night.

I was just beginning the child within work. Each new memory that came would knock me down to emotional depths from which I hope no one else ever has to recover.

By the time I quit the practice I had written close to a thousand prayers in a wide spectrum of categories. Each one helped me connect to my loving Mother God.

I was raised to see God as this white-haired, father-like figure. As a child I imagined Him to look something like the *Wizard of Oz*.

In my reading quest on matters spiritual, I learned that English is the only major language on Earth that fails to ascribe a feminine aspect to our loving God. As painful as the emotional recovery work was for me in dealing with the memories of being sexually assaulted by men, I wanted what I hadn't received as a child.

I found just what I was looking for with my loving Mother God. She is kind, patient, understanding, forgiving, wise, caring and loves you (and me) deeply with Her unconditional love. It is beyond our human ability to create anything like it.

Back then I was a mess. Tears streamed as I wrote prayers, especially prayers written in the category I later named "In the Raw." I called them that because they haven't been revised or edited and fit in the inner child category.

One evening, I wrote a prayer and words came to me I had never heard before. The title was "Robbing the Giver."

Those words startled me. It took me a spell, but as I finally dove through my upbringing, I realized, sadly, that I had done that to more people than I can count, starting at a very early age.

As a child, I did my best to do as I was told. Until I did the work with Sara, I had no idea the effects of my becoming co-dependent by age three had had on me.

Every time I was paid a compliment I deflected and always, always, gave one back. I thought I was doing the right thing. Never once did I stop to consider the impact and affect my doing so had on the person who gave me a compliment.

A few years later came some wisdom unexpectedly. It was when I had those five clients at the Cartmell Home, in Palestine, Texas. The wisdom came as I pondered why all of them were living there.

Three of them I had known since I was a tyke. The late H. Carnathan was like the other two. He'd rather give than receive.

In their generation, they weren't taught emotional truths. Unless I cleaned up my side of the street (my emotional junk) first, then whatever I give to others is tainted. Unfortunately, I gave others what I didn't wish to give them. Think of

Pig-Pen happily living in his own cloud of dust in the comic strip Peanuts.

Suddenly I knew why each one of them was living at the Cartmell Home. It came to me as I drove back to my office following a conference in the small bedroom of one of my clients. Habitual givers, they all had to learn how to receive before they died.

As residents in an extended care facility, they all received daily.

In that moment, I decided that I would learn how to receive with grace before I, too, had to pull on a pair of adult diapers. I had no idea how long such a recovery would take.

Learning to accept a compliment without saying anything but "thank you" took me a long two years. The cause of my not being able to accept a compliment was rooted in the codependent traits I had learned as a young boy.

I was never good enough and couldn't get it right for my parents, Jack and Jackie. Those are just two of the wonderful pieces of emotional baggage I carried as I grew up.

Accepting the first compliment I received without returning one was a huge accomplishment in my life! I was torn to pieces on the inside, even though I knew better.

A bit of wisdom finally came through loudly and with great clarity. My giving a compliment to someone who had complimented me was flat wrong on my part.

Countless times in my life I had robbed the giver of receiving the grace of giving.

Such was never my desire or intention. I've asked forgiveness from each one of them, even though I don't remember all their names any more.

I do remember when my friend, Sandra Lane, complimented me years ago, saying I was wearing a good-looking coat. Sandra is direct and chided me when

I returned her compliment by saying, "Jackson, can't you just accept a compliment?"

Sadly, I missed the chance for self-improvement back then. To say I was clueless in those days is a significant understatement.

As I said, it took a while for me to learn how to feel the grace coming into my body with each compliment I received. I truly had to learn how to appreciate those kind remarks.

Once I finally became comfortable receiving a compliment, I came up with the perfect words to say beyond "thank you." The words affirm the giver's grace.

Now if compelled to say something more than is typical, I simply say, "Thank you - that is so very gracious of you."

If it's someone I know well enough, when I pass along a compliment to them and they say anything other than "Thank you," to me, I challenge them politely. I do so by repeating the compliment I gave to them.

My goal is to get them to shift themselves into gratitude and appreciation.

I have been amazed at how many others have the same difficulty I had accepting compliments. Each time I come across someone who is like what I once was, I pass along my little secret formula to them.

May it work as effectively for them as it has for me.

20

Heart to Heart

I always have had a strong interest in world affairs, even before I was a teenager. Not since 1963, which brought us to and through the Cuban missile crisis unscathed, have I been as concerned for our country and the rest of the world as I am today.

In college I read a book entitled *On The Beach* by Neville Shute. He detailed the end of human life in the world, which started with a nuclear war between two tiny nations as I recall.

Needless to say, one nuclear bomb deserved another in retaliation. It was a frightening book back then, even more so now.

Currently we have three ego-maniacs who hold the key to preserving world peace. They are the president of the United States, Donald Trump, the Supreme Commander of North Korea, Kim Jong-un, and Russian president, Vladimir Putin.

About ten years ago I employed a technique I had learned from Judy Goodman, called "heart to heart."

At the time, the Palestinians and Israelis were locked in tit-for-tat street fighting. Innocent civilian lives were being lost on both sides nearly every day, it seemed.

Along with prayers for peace coming from millions of people, I added my "heart to heart" exercise every day for six weeks. All of a sudden, an enormous shift came and the warring factions put down their arms. Thanks be to God.

"Heart to heart" works in all situations. That's because it calls in the energy of the divine: unconditional love.

As I learned from Sara, human love always has an agenda.

Every time I use the "heart to heart" exercise I feel a shift in my own heart space. I encourage everyone to learn and use this very powerful exercise.

As Judy taught me, all you or I have to do is set our personal protections and bring in our own higher self or soul. Then bring in the person (living or dead) and his/her higher self to be seated about four feet in front of you.

Then use these words:

"Heart to heart, unconditional love, without intention or agenda. Heart to heart, unconditional love."

Judy taught me to repeat what had just been said.

Everyone I know, including myself, benefits from receiving unconditional love. That's because it is the essence of the Divine, without human ego attached to it.

To you, the reader of this chapter, I bring you in and bless you with the powerful heart to heart exercise.

I encourage you to use this exercise on each of the leaders mentioned above.

The more I use this exercise on others, the more pure love I feel in my own heart. The more love I feel in my heart, the more I have to share with others.

Please join me in using this powerful tool. You and I receive just as much as we give away!

21

Learning to Listen

Three years after my dad died I learned a valuable lesson. It felt like a come-uppance at the time, but "oh well," as I have learned to say.

I visited Uncle Clyde and Aunt Howard at their home in Houston. He was a successful businessman in the marine insurance field.

They had business guests for dinner at their home and graciously included me. Somewhere during the evening, the conversation began lagging.

That made me really uncomfortable, so I jumped in with the wisdom and enthusiasm of a teenager. Very shortly Uncle Clyde told me in front of God and their company that, "Jackson, you learn more by listening than by talking."

I don't remember how many more words I spoke that evening. They were the least possible though.

It was not until I hatched from my inner shell that the importance of what my Uncle Clyde told me at such a young age truly sank in. There is great wisdom in developing your listening skills.

Sharpen your listening skills!

When listening, many of us zone out into our ego. That prevents us from being observant and perceiving all we can gather. The person speaking to us says a lot with their body language.

We take ourselves seriously, as if what we have to say are the most important words spoken. As we are busy preparing to respond, we fail to actively listen to what is spoken to us.

There is a fabulous quote which, in my humble opinion, is still true today.

**"Most people do not listen
with the intent to understand.
They listen with the intent to reply."**

Stephen Covey (2001)

As you begin developing your listening skills, listen closely. Observe the person's demeanor and listen to the emotions behind their words. That is regardless of whether their voice is raised or is monotonic.

Culturally, we are steeped in negativity daily. Advertisements let us know we aren't sexy enough, attractive enough, we don't have the right vehicle for success, own the latest gadgets, consume the right food and beverages - it goes on ad nauseam.

Political pundits make hay by spewing toxic opinions of others who have a different point of view from their own. Few realize the pundits are in the entertainment business. The madder they make their audience, the larger their paychecks become.

**Against that setting, I was determined to
change myself. Positive thoughts bring
positive results. This was the same time that I
became determined to learn how to receive a
compliment without robbing the giver.**

Many times, in conversation back then, I felt as if I were Forrest Gump. I would listen to what had been said and there would be a long pause as I formulated my response in a positive fashion. Those empowering words didn't roll off my tongue. I had to discover them one word and one sentence at a time.

I was slower replying than most people I encountered preferred, yet I felt better about my replies, as the energy of the words had changed.

Over time and with daily practice, my response speed became almost normal. I remind myself from time to time, however, about the importance of slowing down.

Using the correct words to reply, even if slowly spoken, is a far better choice than spewing out a reply without pondering its consequence.

Listening is a skill that is never perfected. It can be improved, however, with a personal intent to become a better listener. I do not like or appreciate being interrupted, and feel that no one else does either. Listening is a two-way street.

To listen with the intent to feel and understand what the other person is saying honors them and who they are. It is important that the person speaking not be interrupted.

The more closely I listen without interrupting the more the ladies at Texas First Title Company feel heard.

For me, learning to listen is the same as any other life lesson. It takes the intention to improve and practice for me to become better at it. I still have room for improvement!

22

Experience is What You Get

**"Experience is what you get when you were
expecting something else."**

Anonymous

Just as I began learning universal truths, there always
seemed to be a comeuppance that would show up. I
remember the time when Joe Ed Bunton called me
down at the beginning of a city council meeting about six
weeks after I was elected mayor. I was in charge of running
the council meetings.

Colonel Jack Selden, a previous mayor, had thrown up
his hands and resigned midway through his third term. I
never asked, but am certain it was due to Joe Ed and his
bullying antics.

Jack Selden had written a beautiful welcoming message
to citizens and visitors. He read it before getting to the
council's agenda at each meeting. Joe Ed had a different
idea for me, though.

At the first council meeting in July, I began to read the
welcome. There must have been a grand total of five folks,
other than city staff members, who were attending.

Joe Ed interrupted shortly after I began. He challenged my authority to read the welcoming message. Joe Ed spewed his pent-up anger on whomever he could.

That is an example of having an experience in my life when I was expecting something else. Joe Ed had been courteous to me until that meeting.

Wisdom comes with experience, though. By now, I have lots and lots of experience!

Instinctively, I went to the first item of business on the agenda and followed *Robert's Rules of Order* for the rest of the meeting.

Then there was the time during a council meeting when Ms. Mabel Johnson, a citizen of Palestine who's now deceased, addressed us - as she frequently did. She always had a complaint.

I remember her from when I was a knee-high tyke. She was the check-out clerk at Andy Frantzen's grocery store where my mom always shopped. Ms. Johnson was quick, accurate and friendly as I recall.

Sometimes Jackie would call in her order and they'd deliver it to her door. Somehow the three Frantzen brothers managed to make a decent living out of that store. To my four-year-old self it looked huge. Now, I'm amazed at how small its footprint is.

Back then there was no such thing as pre-packaged cheese. Dutch, the butcher, always had a large wheel of cheddar cheese on hand.

I remember the countless times I went with my mom up to the meat counter where she'd buy the family's meat for the week. Each time Dutch put a couple of slices of cheddar cheese on butcher paper for me.

I always thanked him, as I should. Little did I realize back then how much Dutch's tiny effort meant to me.

Thanks to Joe Ed and his antics at council meetings the council voted to cut back the time for people to speak regarding agenda items. We pared it back from five minutes to three.

On one occasion Mabel went on a rant about what we were doing wrong. I dutifully listened.

During the council meetings, the city attorney served as our time keeper. He informed Mabel that her speaking time was up.

I remember her next words were, "Mayor, I'm not finished speaking yet."

Before I could get a single word out of my mouth, Mike Chennault, a city councilman, retorted, "Rave on, Mabel."

Needless to say, Mabel did just that. She went through the roof and I opted to let her have her say. Our meetings were telecast over the local cable television station, as there was no such thing as satellite television in 1989.

Yes, that was another experience in my tool belt. Somehow, I innately knew that if any one of the CAVE people (Citizens Against Virtually Everything) ever knew they had gotten under my skin, it would be a game-over win for them.

Instead, I followed the standards for meetings and such set by *Robert's Rules of Order* to the letter. I remained courteous to all, even when I wanted to crawl out of my skin. That was because of the ridiculous statements and accusations being made by Joe Ed and his supporters on the council.

Mine your experiences for the wisdom hidden in them!

Experiences shaped me into who I am today. I'm better than I was before. That's because I finally started digging through the obvious to find the wisdom contained in each experience.

I still have lots of room for improvement though.

23

Walk Around the Block

As I've written, my Uncle Clyde had great wisdom, though sometimes he was gruff when he delivered it. I caught a piece of it in the summer of 1977, just after I graduated from Bates College of Law at the University of Houston.

My law school classmates and I studied harder than any of us ever had studied before that summer. We had an enormous amount of material to read and digest to ready ourselves to answer all of the questions on the upcoming bar exam.

Those who passed it were able to obtain their law license and be sworn in by a judge or magistrate. I was in the lucky category.

In truth there is no test I had ever taken that compared to what the bar examiners threw at us. The first day was called the "multi-state" test, which we took over a six-hour period.

The questions were true/false. My classmates and I mused that had we studied for a plumber's license we would have felt better about our answers.

The second day we were given essay exams over many categories and topics on Texas law. It was an eight-hour day of thinking and coming up with the best answers we could, in prose form.

I spent each day that summer at Uncle Clyde and Aunt Howard's house on West Broad Oak Street in Houston. Only for meals and to help clean up did I leave my study room. My life was preparing for the exam.

Day after day, week after week, it was the same routine. Then at supper one evening, out of Uncle Clyde's mouth came these words, "Jackson, go outside and walk around the block."

I knew better than to protest my host's directive. It was a hot, humid evening in Houston, typical for late June.

Walking around the block shifts everything for me!

By the time I returned I had realized the wisdom Uncle Clyde had given me. A ten-minute walk refreshed my mind, shifted my energy and completely changed my perspective. It also helped improve my attitude.

I was grateful for his wisdom and from that day began taking study-break walks when my mind and body grew weary.

Fast forward twenty-five years. I modified Uncle Clyde's suggestion and always employed its derivation with humor.

Many times, when a title company employee became frustrated, I would walk them to the front of the building. Then we'd go outside and walk around the front porch support posts. Doing so took them away from the desk for a few minutes.

Each time their result was the same as mine was back in 1977. Getting up from your desk and going outside can have a magical impact on your frame of mind!

To this day, I get up from my desk and go outside at least twice an hour during work days. Doing so always shifts my perspective and freshens my attitude toward what I am working on.

24

A Frozen Sponge

In 2001, we were still adding scanned documents to our digitized title data base. We had an employee scan images of pages in the bound books located in the basement of the county clerk's office.

Those images would then be transferred onto a disk, and uploaded into our halFile program at Texas First Title Company. Next, an employee would index the critical information found in each document.

For a title plant (our computerized data base) to be licensed by the Texas Department of Insurance, we must index instruments by names of grantors and grantees. We also must index each instrument geographically.

That means we have to index the legal description by subdivision with lot and block numbers. For rural property we must index the legal description by survey name(s) and acreage amounts.

One morning our courthouse scanning computer died. I remember what happened next as if it had happened earlier today.

I went to the courthouse basement and removed all of the wired connections to the peripheral equipment from the computer. I remember bending over to pick the computer up off the floor to return it to the title company office. As I lifted the machine, which wasn't heavy, it felt as if a large branch in my back snapped in two. The breath was knocked out of me for a few seconds.

Once I began breathing normally again, I tried taking a normal step. That didn't work at all. So tiny step by tiny step I made the trek up the stairs and across the street to the title company office.

An elderly man who can only manage to shuffle his feet forward could travel faster than I did that morning.

Though it was only 8:30 in the morning, I knew my work day was finished. I had never felt the pain from a back spasm before but experienced it intensely that day.

I had been getting weekly massages from Becky, who had been a registered nurse for years, and a super good one at that. The first time Becky worked on my shoulders she likened them to working with a piece of steel,

I was so uptight that I didn't even have the courage to remove my shirt. I did so for the second appointment and that made an enormous difference as Becky was able to dig more deeply to help get stress out of my shoulders.

Back then, I confess I was way too formal and uptight. I even wore heavily starched white cotton shirts! My close friends commented that I was a type AAAA personality, which I don't deny.

That morning I called Becky, who lived near Slocum, Texas, and let her know I was in need of her help right away.

Somehow, I managed to drive myself to her home, some twenty minutes away. When I told her what happened, she chided me and said it would have been better for me to go home and lie prone instead of going to see her.

I asked if going to a chiropractor would help. Her immediate response was" NO! Not now." Only after 72 hours' rest should one even touch my lower back after it acted up.

Though I didn't receive the immediate help I desired, Becky gave me a bit of wisdom I still use from time to time. She told me to get a fresh sponge and fill it with water until it's full but not dripping. Then I was to place it in a Ziploc bag and freeze it.

I made it home and did just as Becky told me. My job was to put the frozen sponge directly on the middle of my lower back for fifteen minutes every hour.

My feet never made it faster than shuffling speed that day, but the sponge gave me some immediate relief which was greatly welcomed!

Within a couple of days, my gait was back to normal. I was frustrated and embarrassed that I had missed a day's work because of something that sounds innocuous - a back spasm.

About seven years later, I needed to go through a title company file to see if I could solve a problem we had with it. The file was more than four inches thick in a legal sized file with two dividers.

I crossed my legs and opened the file on my lap. Instantly I felt my lower back snap.

This time my body gave me a different reaction. Though I felt the pain in my lower back, my body quit breathing. I didn't know if I was having a heart attack, for I couldn't take in a breath for thirty seconds.

Finally, I was able to get air into my lungs. I had never known what a blessing just being able to breathe is!

**My back spasms were caused
by psychological reasons.**

This time I took the time to look up "Lower Back Problems" in an amazing book authored by Dr. Michael J. Lincoln, Ph.D. (1991, 4ᵗʰ Rev. 2006, p. 93). It's in dictionary form and is entitled *Messages From The Body*.

I have worked with it many, many times since I purchased my first copy. His assessments of the root cause of a tremendous number of aches, pains, dis-eases, broken bones and the like are amazing.

When I find the right category or root cause for whatever is going on in my body, his description hits me right between the eyes each time. He's very hard on family of origin, but so be it.

That's where most of my "dis-eases" started. As I learned from an article I read last fall, "Our childhood stays with us forever."

Dr. Lincoln let me know with certainty the reason why my back snapped into a spasm. It was because I didn't feel emotionally supported in my life or endeavors. When both spasms occurred, he was deadly accurate.

I am extremely fortunate to live the life I do. I am even more fortunate to have wonderful people help me from time to time.

I have learned now to feel the beginnings of a back spasm coming on. I remind myself of the reason why it is acting up, then put myself in a different emotional place by shifting out of frustration and into gratitude and appreciation.

Thanks to Becky's wisdom, I also give my lower back what relieves it quickly - the frozen sponge.

Hint: I keep a frozen sponge in both my home and office refrigerator's freezer compartment at all times.

25

Resentment Power

The title company was hit hard by the 2008 recession caused by a financial instrument I had never heard of, "credit default swaps."

By April of 2009, something inside me changed. The impact happened when I believed I was as healthy as the proverbial horse. Out of the blue I became woozy and saw stars when I arose from the prone position of sleep.

Those same stars appeared in my field of vision when I stood up after tying my tennis shoes I wore to do my yard work. The stars resembled those I had seen as a child when a television cartoon character was bopped on the head.

After a month, the symptoms hadn't disappeared, so I knew something was amiss. I made an appointment to see Edith Mitchell, in Palestine.

A certified herbalist and nutritionist, Edith also does stress reductions and muscle testing. The latter is applied kinesiology, a pseudo-scientific practice. She is an amazing practitioner and is highly intuitive.

I've sent many title company employees who were dealing with health issues to her. Each one's health, ranging from being cold all the time to a cough that wouldn't go away, improved. All of them, and I too, sing her high praises!

She's helped me release emotional trauma from being sabotaged at work as well as helped me deal with my work stress. Years ago she helped me quickly recover from a nearly blown-out Achilles' tendon.

In my appointment to start getting rid of seeing "stars" she discerned that I had a 49% arterial blockage. Edith described the symptoms I was experiencing without asking me any questions.

I wanted to avoid taking blood thinner meds for the rest of my life, so I opted to explore alternatives. Uncle Clyde took Coumadin (think rat poison – the same substance we put out to control rodents, and which caused the death of Pepper, the sweetest dog I've ever had) for something like twenty years before he died. I observed what it did to his skin and didn't want the same for my body.

Edith suggested I start my day with early-morning walks. I improved my diet and began losing a bit of weight, and each day I took the supplements she had recommended.

A month later, by muscle testing my wrist during a re-check session, she discerned that the blockage had decreased by a whopping one percent. Armed with a second set of supplements, I went another month before checking in with Edith again.

In the interim, I made an appointment to see my good friend and award-winning practitioner, Frankie Burget. Her practice is in the Dallas-Fort Worth area.

I had worked with Frankie on many of the same days I did the child within work with Sara several years before. Frankie is a myofascial therapist (among the many modalities in which she is licensed). As I tell folks, with tongue in cheek, she has more certifications on the walls of her office than Heinz has ketchup labels.

The first words out of Frankie's mouth when she walked into the exam room were, "Jackson, you're holding on to a resentment." I belly laughed out loud and told Frankie she was exactly right.

At the time, I was holding onto buried emotional feelings regarding my mom. They arose for me when she moved into an extended-care facility, never to return home again.

The reason for my laughter is that what I learned in twelve-step work immediately kicked in. For whatever reason, I had to experience what happens to our hearts when we carry such emotional burdens.

In twelve-step work I learned that expectations bear the seeds of resentment. As I had attended plenty of Al-Anon meetings years before, I knew better than to bear resentment toward anyone.

**Until released, resentments owned my mind,
body and soul.**

In the hour's appointment, Frankie unlocked the energetic bucket in which I had buried all the Jackie resentments. My body twisted and contorted on the exam table as Frankie helped my physical body and my energetic self release all of the Jackie resentments I had been holding onto.

The next morning, as I arose from prone to standing after my night's sleep, there were no stars in my field of vision. I felt more chipper, too.

With Frankie's appointment behind me, I scheduled a follow-up visit with Edith. A couple of weeks later she muscle tested my wrist to determine where on the scale of 1 to 100 my arterial blockage was.

She stopped at nineteen and said that was the percentage of arterial blockage I had then, and that it was about normal for a man my age.

**Resentments can be powerful.
They hurt our hearts in a very real way.**

It is important for our physical health to release them before they do irreversible damage to our heart or cardiovascular system.

Thank you, Edith and Frankie, for being the amazing people you are. Double thanks to Frankie for calling out what she saw and for helping my body release the Jackie resentments I had buried.

That experience was an enormous wake-up call for me about the power resentments have.

26

The Power of Forgiveness

Forgiving others has always been easy for me. In fact, for many years, I wondered why forgiving others was so hard for other people.

By age three, I had figured out that I was responsible for whatever was wrong at home, in my parents' lives, and more. It was always my fault, even if I had done nothing wrong.

I've mused that when a puff of a cloud appeared on an otherwise cloudless day, I surely must have done something wrong. That's a sick sign of codependent traits in a child, I've learned.

Thanks to Sara, the wisdom and the exercises she gave me to do years ago helped me release much of the guilt I carried. Finally, I'm almost guilt-free.

As for forgiveness, Sara gave me a physical exercise to do, toward the very end of my child within work with her. I was stunned by the outcome.

To me, the exercise was ridiculously simple. I thought so, even though Sara had told me how personally powerful it was for her when she did the very same exercise years before.

Nevertheless, off to Lowe's I went to buy a couple of pieces of plastic piping. With the pipe in hand, I drove out into the country, well away from town.

My friend, Gay Fuller, allowed me to go deep into the woods on her property. It was early in the afternoon on a typical August summer afternoon in East Texas. That means the humidity was about sixty percent and the temperature was over one hundred degrees, with no breeze.

I walked across her property until I was far from civilization. No human could see or hear me, even if I yelled for help.

In my lawyer's mind, I could not imagine what power there would be in whacking a piece of plastic pipe against a tree. I had no idea what Sara and a tree on my friend's property had to teach me.

As I walked past the pasture toward the woods, I found the right tree, a tall oak tree with a trunk about three feet in diameter. I asked its permission for me to flail away at it, which was instantly granted.

I gave the pipe a mighty heave and to my surprise, it shattered into pieces. I was shocked! Surely the old oak tree was laughing at me.

Thinking I had used a defective piece of pipe, I swung the second piece of pipe against the innocent tree. The same thing happened.

Obviously I had to come up with a completely different plan, so I found branches of the tree that had fallen to the ground.

When I found the right-sized one, I again asked permission of the old oak tree. Again, permission was granted quickly.

With the correct tree branch in hand, I flailed away at the trunk of the tree. I sought to whack and hurt all of those men who had sexually abused me as a child. The mighty oak tree never budged.

I swung at least as hard seeking to return the favor to my mother. She had beaten me as a small child with her favorite mahogany-colored bat. She also used her hands, and of course, the iron skillet which she used to hit me upside the head.

The harder I swung the tree's branches at its trunk, the greater my failure. Soon my tears of failure became rivers streaming down my face. That was when I finally learned one of the lessons Sara intended me to.

Through my deepest, sobbing tears, I forgave all of the perpetrators. I did so regardless of what they had done to me as a child. Yet something was still missing.

As I dug deeper, I quickly realized there was another person for me to forgive. That person was *me*. That is because as long as I held onto the feelings that I had for those whom I remembered abusing me in childhood, those monsters would continue to own me night and day.

**I untied myself from those who hurt me
by forgiving them, and me.**

When I finally forgave myself, more gut-wrenching tears streamed down my perspiring face. With Sara's exercise, I had learned the second lesson she intended for me.

**Sara, and the wise oak tree I found in the
middle of nowhere on that hot August Texas
afternoon, gifted me with two of the most
powerful lessons I've learned in my lifetime.**

**They are the importance of forgiving others
and the importance of forgiveness of self.**

That August afternoon I released many layers of my buried feelings. I also released a lot of the physical pain, shame, guilt, anger, disappointments, frustrations and regrets of my childhood past.

By forgiving them, and myself too, I finally untied myself from those who had hurt me so badly.

27

Blankets and Bears

My good friend, Joe Coleman, and I came up with an idea. It was 2007 and we lived in a rural community of 19,000 people.

Joe has been president of the Anderson County Child Welfare Board for many of the last twenty years. He doesn't crave power, he just wants things done properly to best benefit the children in our county who desperately need a helping hand.

Being president of that board is a thankless job. There's never enough money nor enough trained folks to take care of all the needs of the underprivileged children here.

Joe and I had the idea of starting a small non-profit fund we named Blankets and Bears. Our initial thought was to raise money to purchase new stuffed animals and blankets to give to children who had been abused, traumatized, or sexually assaulted.

Blankets and Bears got off to a bit of a slow start because asking people and business folks for money was not a strong suit for either of us. I have mused more than once that if I had to make a living as a salesman, I'd be homeless.

Within a few years, Sandra Lane joined our volunteer group. The only criterion to join the group as a volunteer was to care about the welfare and well-being of children.

Sandra knocked our group into shape quickly. She was very well organized and successful at fundraising, too!

With Sandra's help, Blankets and Bears took off. We went from raising a pittance at our annual fundraiser to being very successful. That came from the generous caring folks in our community.

A new volunteer showed up, Jessi Jones, the Sexual Assault Nurse Examiner at Palestine Regional Memorial Hospital.

She and her husband, Craig Jones, were active in their church, Court Drive Church of Christ. Its pastor, Paul Jones (no relation to Jessi and Craig), gets more direct service hours out of his church members than any other church in our area. That's my opinion, at least.

Our group was sitting on a bank account with more than $25,000.00 in it, but until Jessi showed up none of us had any idea which organizations best served the abused children in our community.

At one of the first meetings Jessi attended, I happened to ask her if there was anything we could do for her. She informed us that the forensic examination equipment she used was old and outdated. Sometimes she would have to take the examination pictures with her cell phone. Those pictures often ended up as evidence if the perpetrator's case went to trial.

I asked Jessi how much a new forensic exam table would cost. She let us know that a good, used examination table would run around $12,500.00.

Then I asked how much a new forensic examination table would cost. I wanted to know because sexual assault victims who ended up seeing Jessi were at the most vulnerable time in their lives. In my opinion, those children deserved the best! Jessi told us she would check into it.

At the next meeting, Jessi let us know that a new forensic examination table would cost $25,000.00. The vote was fast and unanimous.

Folks in our community had given generously so we could help children who had been sexually assaulted or otherwise traumatized.

We communicated with the CEO of Palestine Regional Medical Center. He had the hospital make arrangements to buy the new equipment with funds donated by our organization.

During a banquet, Jessi and other volunteers presented a dummy check in the sum of $25,000.00 to the hospital's community board.

Once the forensic equipment arrived and Jessi was trained to use it, she began her forensic exams with state-of-the-art equipment.

The hospital had put Jessi in a small room that had no decorations whatsoever. It was as cold and unfriendly as could be.

Jessi had artistic talent and came by it naturally, as both her mother and grandmother are artists.

Jessi came up with an idea and brought poster boards and paint to our next meeting. Then she obtained hand prints from our volunteers.

She also acquired hand prints from folks who worked the cases she handled. They included the district attorney and investigators in his office, and other adults who became involved with sexual-assault victims in their professional careers.

Our hand prints were multi-colored and used as leaves on branches of a tree Jessi had drawn. By the time she finished collecting hand prints there were lots of leaves on the tree.

Jessi used that poster board to let children she examined know there were lots of adults who are safe to be around. The children also learned that there are good adults who sincerely care for their well-being. And... Jessi was working on another idea.

She drew another tree on a second piece of poster board. This time she obtained hand prints from those whom she examined on her new table.

That tree let every child she interviewed and examined know that there are many other children who have had the same horrific experiences they had. Being a member of that group, I know those trees were meaningful to every single victim Jessi interviewed.

A couple of years later, Jessi had Becky Cunio come talk to us at one of our meetings. Becky worked at the Palestine office of the Crisis Center of Cherokee and Anderson County.

Jessi already knew, but Becky showed us pictures of the interview room they used for the sexual assault victims. My opinion was that a drop-off room at a rundown thrift store would be more comforting than that room at the Crisis Center.

I was embarrassed that our community couldn't do better for the victims, especially children and teenagers. Others were too.

We asked how much it would cost to renovate the room. Beckie let us know that a couple of thousand dollars would do. I sensed that the sum mentioned would be a temporary solution and not one we would be proud of.

At the next meeting we voted to give the Crisis Center $5,000.00, which Jessi said would transform the room. Indeed, it did!

Jessi and Craig donated flooring material and labor. New furniture was purchased. The camera law enforcement officials used to view and listen to the victims being interviewed was much better hidden.

After the renovations were made, we heard from other communities that they said they wished they had a room just like ours.

In 2015 we learned that more than thirty percent of the children in our county miss at least one meal per day. To me that is another inexcusable form of child abuse.

One of Paul Jones' ministries is to feed adults who are in true need and not simply looking for a hand out. He and his volunteers screen them before approving them.

Once a week, they feed more than 275 people in the church's community room. The facility's kitchen is small, as is their storage area.

Regardless of the size, they pull it off successfully each week. As Paul and his volunteers feed children, as well as adults, we decided to help them that year.

We had raised enough funds to donate $10,000.00 to the Palestine Community Food Pantry. Our donation helped them buy a larger cooler as well as the concrete slab for it to sit on.

This allowed Paul's group to provide fresh eggs and vegetables to those whom they served. The things we take for granted are overwhelming when we stop and think about them.

Over the years, Blankets and Bears has brought awareness to our community as well. We invited Jon Holsten, a former detective and policeman with the Fort Collins, Colorado, police force to make an appearance in Palestine.

Jon wrote the book *The Swimsuit Lesson*. It's a book to be read to children, showing which parts of their body are not to be touched by a non-parent or care giver.

At the back of the book is a primer. Jon emphasizes the importance of discussing inappropriate touching with children. He also speaks of the importance of children telling parents the truth if it ever happens.

For many years, the local Walmart Distribution Centers 6005 and 6036 have generously contributed to our cause, through Walmart Foundation, Inc., its non-profit arm. Plus numerous employees at the Palestine Walmart Distribution

Center 6005 have donated stuffed animals and blankets to our organization. The gifts come from true working-class folks, many of whom have hearts of gold.

We deliver them to the Crisis Center, our community SANE (Sexual Assault Nurse Examiner), the district attorney's crime victim's advocate, CASA, the Palestine Police Department and other organizations.

Our small organization provides bandages for children in our community who have been abused, traumatized and/or sexually assaulted. It sickens me, but national statistics say that by the time they reach eighteen years of age twenty-five percent of all females and one in six boys will have been sexually assaulted.

From my personal experience I know two things about children who have been sexually assaulted.

From the moment it happens, life is forever changed for a child/adolescent/adult who is sexually assaulted.

First, their lives have forever changed and there is no going back. Second, they'll never totally overcome all of the impacts that being sexually assaulted causes.

That said, thanks be to all of the Blankets and Bears volunteers who care. Kudos and super thanks to all who have donated and contributed to the cause.

Maybe it's just a band-aid, but my hope is that the stuffed animals and blankets we distribute help survivors recover, knowing that in their worst moments someone cares for them.

28

The Perfect Response

Jackie had lived at Sterling House, an assisted-living facility, for a couple of years. She tolerated her existence there, but certainly didn't go out of her way to be sociable.

Instead of being grateful for having something to eat, she lamented that the food just wasn't good. It must be hell on Earth to give up all the earthly freedoms you once had as an adult.

Early one afternoon, I received a call from Debbie, the assistant to the director at Sterling House.

She let me know she had something to tell me about my mom. I expected the worst.

That afternoon I was insanely busy, just as I had been all morning. I had law office clients to take care of and triage opportunities at the title company.

Debbie informed me that she had caught Jackie's arm in a cocked position during the noon meal. Jackie was about to launch her plate full of food at another resident.

Needless to say, I stopped what I was doing and went to see my feeble mom. I told her what Debbie had told me and asked if it were true.

Jackie's denial was that she would never do such a thing. Of course she wouldn't - in her own mind. She never once owned up to anything I remember her doing to me as a child.

For the first time in my life, I told Jackie my truth. I let her know that she had a choice to make.

In no uncertain terms, I let Jackie know what she did going forward was a choice, and she'd have to live with its consequences.

She could continue on the path she was on. By doing so she'd have no one to come sit with her at mealtimes and would become totally isolated at Sterling House. Her other choice was to pull her charm out of its box and start using it so she would be the best-liked-resident there.

When I returned to the office, I called my good friend, Steve Presley. As he's a pharmacist, I felt certain he'd know if Jackie's behavior was a sign of future problems going forward.

I told him about the incident at Sterling House as if it were deadly serious. It certainly was to me.

Steve guffawed and let me know those are commonplace occurrences at assisted-living and long-term care facilities. I was shocked!

At the time, I had not yet discerned the perfect response I could have used with my mom. Back then, Steve and his sweet wife, Cindi, hosted Steve's mom at their house. Grace Billy took up residence at their house when she was recovering from a serious surgery. It was easier for them to care for her at their home instead of at her house. Not many adults I know would do as much for an elderly family member as Steve and Cindi did.

As Grace Billy recovered, she regained her tenacious wits about her. I had learned many years earlier that it was easier to accede to her requests than not.

She'd simply beat you down with a stream of words that made you feel awful if you didn't do as she requested.

A few years later I received a call from Steve. Grace Billy had started treating him and Cindi as if their home had become hers. By golly, things were going to be done HER way.

I only can imagine the frustration, disappointment and angst Steve and Cindi lived with daily. Steve asked if I had any ideas that might help.

Then I let him know what I now refer to as the perfect response for situations like that, and many others too. I told him to use these words with Grace Billy the next time she made her demands.

"That doesn't work for me at this time."

I suggested to Steve that he use that sentence and then turn around and walk out of the room.

The sentence is direct, it's the truth, and it sets a boundary. No explanation is needed as clear boundaries are set.

Steve later told me that his mother's response was silence. Afterward, he said, Grace Billy began treating him and Cindi with the respect and appreciation they truly deserved.

"That doesn't work for me at this time."

Jackson Hanks

That simple sentence levels an uneven playing field, giving the innocent ones a fair chance.

29

IHSS

Not to be confused with ISIS, IHSS is a disease of the human heart. It stands for Idiopathic Hypertrophic Subaortic Stenosis.

My dear friend, the late Father Clay Piatt, was the priest at St. Phillip's Episcopal Church in Palestine, Texas, when he died from that disease at the tender age of forty-three on June 6, 1989.

Prior to selecting Father Clay as its rector, the church had sent out search committees to interview and return with information to its local governing body, the vestry. The search was necessary due to the death of our former priest, Father Joe Routh.

The late Dr. Harvey Bell, a retired physician, was scheduled to go with me to visit Father Clay Piatt and his wife, Suzy. At the time, Father Clay was the priest of the Episcopal Church in Hitchcock, Texas.

As Dr. Bell decided not to make the trek, I did so by myself. There was no instruction manual. Rather, there were suggestions from other search committee members who had already interviewed other candidates.

I will always remember my visit with Clay and Suzy at their home. Clay smoked a pipe, and both he and his wife were friendly and cordial.

Father Clay had a depth to his wisdom, and a deep voice, too. I knew from the moment I met him that I had met a special man.

That impression was strongly confirmed the next morning as I attended his church's early Sunday morning service. The ten-minute sermon he preached covered uncommon topics delivered with wisdom.

The vestry made its call and Father Clay Piatt became St. Phillip's new priest. Sadly, his family had a tragedy occur the day they were to move to Palestine.

Their teenaged son, Warren Piatt, died during the night. He had suffered from the same disease as his dad did.

St. Phillip's was fortunate to have Father Clay as its priest for the time he was there. Not only did Father Clay have wisdom, he also had a wonderful sense of humor.

I still remember the time he and Suzy came to our home for the celebratory Easter meal. My mom was there, and I was stunned during the feast - Father Clay taught us all how to hang a spoon on our noses. Jackie not only participated but also laughed at our successes and failures, including her own!

A year after Father Clay died, I went to the local Kroger's grocery store early one morning to buy an item for the office. All of a sudden, as I walked out of the store to my car, the scent of his pipe smoke was present - it was just as if I had been in his office.

I knew that he was in a good place and smiled at his reminder. Clay and Suzy were kind, caring and loving to our young daughters.

It was two years later that I had a full physical. I was healthy, or so I thought. I was sent to what was then Memorial Hospital in Palestine for an EKG. Dr. Thomas Glenn, a radiologist with the hospital, read it and gave me the diagnosis.

He told me that I had IHSS. My dad had died at age forty-seven from a heart attack. I took the news super hard, as with that diagnosis, I wasn't sure I would even make it to forty-seven.

With high cholesterol and heart-disease history on my dad's side of the family, I went super heart-healthy with my diet. I found a book of wisdom with great recipes that were tasty, *Don't Eat Your Heart Out* by Dr. Joseph Piscatella.

He taught the importance of reading labels on products and how to determine the true fat content as a percentage of calories.

I put down table salt and switched to seasoning with different types of peppercorns. In time, I grew a new appreciation for their flavorings.

A couple of summers later I made an appointment to see Susanna Garrison's cardiologist in Houston. He ran me through his battery of tests, including not only an EKG but also an echocardiogram.

When his office called me the next week, I thought I was prepared for whatever they told me the results were. In truth, I was not.

A healthy diet and daily exercise are life preservers for me.

According to the doctor, and those who read my test results, I did not have IHSS or any other heart disease. He recommended I stick with my heart-healthy diet and get plenty of exercise. Not only have I managed to outlive my dad, but I've also now out-lived his dad.

I didn't seek psychological help from anyone back when I received the diagnosis. Nor had Dr. Emoto's books been written about the power and importance of gratitude.

My early mis-diagnosis was a hard blessing in disguise, leading me to be more physically active and practice eating heart-healthy foods.

I started the practice in my mid-thirties and continue to do so. Giving up the fat-based, fried foods I grew up on in East Texas and changing to a heart-healthy diet was the best thing I could do for my body then, and continues to be so.

30

Abandonment

L ittle did I know that as a tyke I had developed abandonment issues. As I wrote about my first term at Camp Rio Vista, they surfaced in overwhelming quantity.

There were several times when my boyhood friends would invite me to spend the night at their home. Often I would dissolve into inconsolable tears before bedtime and my mom would come and pick me up. I was five or six at the time.

You might think I would have relished the chance to have a sleep over at a friend's house. Getting out of my hell on Earth should have been a welcome change.

A few times I braved it and made it safely to the next morning.

And I learned that abandonment triggers are powerful for others, too.

A lady client told the story about her rheumatoid fever as a child. She was hospitalized for several days and nights. As a result, she had horrific abandonment issues that impacted her strongly as an adult.

She had a wonderful childhood and had parents who wanted to spend the night at the hospital with her, but were not allowed to because of hospital protocol.

For the rest of my life, I will always remember what I learned from Sara.

"Abandonment feels like death to a child."

Sara Hays

To me, death is a well-known friend. My ego would rather deal with something familiar than something new. I understand death, as I do the recovery process from its impact. It's just five steps, even though they take time.

Death can trigger abandonment feelings as they did when my dad died. The big "A" was triggered again when Carmen let me know our relationship was over.

I was disconsolate. She was the best friend I had ever had back then.

Carmen was book-smart, wise, caring, considerate, loving and had many other wonderful traits. At the time I was just learning the vocabulary of feelings, thanks to her.

She had what felt like a Ph.D. in feelings, as she would express herself eloquently about them. In turn, she'd ask how I was feeling and at first my responses were typical for an untrained man. It was either, "good," "not too good," "wonderful" or "bad."

In dealing with the loss of my close companion and best friend, I started digging into my tiny bag of feelings. I was beginning to feel and verbalize them. I walked around the courthouse square one morning, hiding my tears.

I asked my angels to wrap their loving wings around me as I was utterly disconsolate. My hope was that they'd keep me from falling to the bottom of the human emotional abyss that morning.

I knew my angels were present, as somehow I felt lighter by the end of my quick walk.

That morning was different for me, though. I kept asking what word to associate with the emotional pain I felt. The word "abandonment" came to my mind.

That was a very tiny step forward in my emotional recovery, yet it was the first feeling word that I searched for and found on my own. That gave me the courage to start finding more of them.

I wasn't taught to feel as a child, or to learn to put words with feelings. Back then, boys were expected to climb trees and to be tough.

Jack would tell me to, "be a man," "men don't cry," "have a stiff upper lip," and other shaming words to toughen me up.

The next year, Margie, the woman whom I dated after Carmen, suggested that I buy and read a copy of a wonderful book called *Feelings Buried Alive Never Die* by Carole Truman. The book was a bit of a slow read for me, but I gained wisdom from it.

In the book's appendix, she lists numerous words for negative feelings. Then she pairs them with our desired positive feelings. It is a powerful list that I still refer to from time to time.

Abandonment was one of life's hardest emotional issues for me to overcome.

It was during the writing of this book that I realized abandonment issues remained with me. Though invisible, they deeply troubled me, so I decided it was time to clear them out for good.

I had a session with Frankie, my myofascial therapist, during October 2017. I let her know at the beginning of our session that dealing with my issues related to abandonment were target number one.

It took a bit of time to get there. Then she intuited where I had hidden them. She saw them inside my chest and lungs, appearing as a heavy set of books weighing me down. Their presence, since childhood, had adversely affected my posture. It seems that my shoulders always seem to be pulled forward, according to Frankie.

She questioned me as to who caused my abandonment issues. In the past, that sort of question would stump me.

This time the answer came with ease. It was Jackie, my mom.

Frankie's myofascial touch is beyond incredible. She had me breathe deeply and put creative visualization to work.

After what seemed like a long time, I finally rid myself of those heavy books that compressed my chest. I released the hideous abandonment issues that had been with me since childhood and an enormous invisible weight was released from my soul.

I also released that which kept me connected to Jackie.

Thanks to Frankie's amazing talents, touch and wisdom, I conquered the abandonment issues that had haunted me for years.

31

Shoulder Shrugging and Eye Rolling

Once Texas First Title Company was licensed by the Texas Department of Insurance and as we started operations, I had many more duties than running my law office. I was the manager of the company and title examiner for each title company file.

As we grew busier, I found that I had to hurry in many new ways. I was (and still am) board certified by the Texas Board of Legal Specialization in Farm & Ranch law and in Residential Real Estate law.

My law office work product had to grade an A+ or A before it went out the door. Though that was my intention with the title company, I learned it wasn't possible. As long as a title company file graded at least an A-, it had to be pushed out the door. That's because in Texas the title company is not paid anything unless the file closes.

That means that even by running a title, examining each instrument in the chain and preparing the commitment, we aren't paid a dime. The only payment we receive for such incomplete files is having an experience.

Each job in the title company office is rewarding, although stressful at times. I'm embarrassed by one of the former traits I showed when I was stressed.

My former companion, Carmen, helped when she could when she came to town. Her home, though, was in Oklahoma.

She told me that I shrugged my shoulders and rolled my eyes whenever an employee asked for help. In my mind, I had a plan and each step I took had a purpose.

My impatience hurt them and ended up hurting me. It seemed like every time I walked through the title company I was a fish - every employee I walked by needed something from me.

They would throw their hooks at me and reel me into whatever their situation was at the time. Carmen let me know that I was being dismissive of my employees when I rolled my eyes and/or shrugged my shoulders. I was totally embarrassed - but she was right.

It took time for me to correct my behavior. I know now that I had been dismissive in the rest of my relationships too.

My eye rolling and shoulder shrugging was dismissive of others.

I've learned to be more patient and tolerant of people. More importantly, I learned the value of active listening.

I'm not nearly as important as I once thought I was.

32

Codependency's Power

In August 2017, I was writing an article and needed a quote on codependent traits. I searched and found a profound one written by Darlene Lancer, a practicing marriage and family therapist (LMFT).

I was so touched by her wisdom that I purchased two books she wrote; *Conquering Shame and Codependency: 8 Steps to Freeing the True You* and *Codependency for Dummies*. The second book is part of the "Dummies" series.

When I began reading the first book, I wasn't ready to delve into the emotional depths of her 8-step program. Life was moving too fast for me at the time.

A couple of weeks after I put down the first book I began reading *Codependency for Dummies*. Chapter after chapter I read, sinking deeper and deeper emotionally as I went.

I wasn't reading for her content or wisdom.

**I was reading about the deep
emotional mess I had been.**

That's when my mind started remembering how I felt about my past.

It was like starting at the top of an emotional roller coaster, reaching the tipping point and then going downhill fast with no brakes to slow me down. With each day, I sank another layer lower in my funk.

The fault wasn't the author's. I take personal responsibility for my emotional well-being.

I've read several of Melanie Beattie's books, including *Codependent No More, Beyond Codependency* and *The Language of Letting Go*. Each contained wisdom that helped me.

I was honestly astonished by the depth and totality of Darlene's wisdom. Her words took me back to my truly messed-up childhood.

Though I hadn't met her, from time to time as I read, I felt as if she had been walking in my shoes, at least part of the time I was growing up.

By the time I finished reading *Codependency for Dummies* I was an emotional wreck, but masked it so others couldn't see beyond the veneer of my presence.

Just as I sank to my emotional bottom, I happened across a short piece that had been posted on Facebook.

The article was entitled *Twenty-Five Traits of Adults Who Had Been Emotionally Abused as a Child.* It was mid-morning when I read the short article and list of traits.

Though it was a super busy morning, I locked the outside door to my law office and put my phone on do not disturb. It's been years since I wept as deeply as I did that morning. I had at least four-fifths of those traits deeply ingrained in me.

A couple of days later, I called on my grit. I had an appointment to see Sara in ten days.

I began re-reading *Codependency for Dummies*. In the second read I was able to absorb Darlene's wisdom of cause and effect without reliving my past. Each chapter helped me better understand who I am and why I sometimes act the way I do.

It reminded me of an experience from 2001. Before my first appointment, Sara had told me to buy a copy of Claudia

Black's book *It Will Never Happen to Me*. In that short book I learned more about myself than my conscious mind had been aware of for the first forty-seven years of my life.

Claudia's wisdom was like Sara's to me. As hard as it was to read early in my recovery process, her book was a game-changer for me.

Darlene's book, and the article, shook my emotions to their very core. I rely on myself as my support system, and when challenged, I reach out to Sara for a dose of her wisdom.

So I was glad when it was time for my hour-and-a-half drive to Winnsboro to see Sara. I took a copy of *Codependency for Dummies* with me, as well as the article.

When the appointment started, I let Sara know how I had slid to the bottom emotionally from reading the book and article. I gave Sara a copy of the book, as she loves to read and learn.

Then I gave her a copy of the article's list of traits. I didn't know what to expect next.

As Sara read through the list, I began to see a twinkle in her eye. By the time she was finished reading, her eyes were gleaming. She was howling and laughing hard, too.

Sara commented on the excellence of the list. Then she said, "Jackson, this list is the person I met when we first started working together, but you aren't that person anymore."

Once again, her wisdom went straight to the bull's-eye. It's so easy for me, as a recovering codependent, to revert to my past behavior instead of celebrating my successes.

Sara knew I had worked hard to overcome nearly all of the traits deeply embedded in me. And... there are a few I'm still working on to overcome.

Codependent traits are just as insidious as other forms of abuse. The article summed it up better than any words I could write:

"Our childhood stays with us forever, and for those who were emotionally abused growing up, that can be a nightmare. Emotional abuse leaves lasting scars that some people never recover from. It can even lead to mental illness and relationship problems."

https://www.peacequarters.com/
25-things-adult-youve-experienced-childhood-
emotional-abuse/

I owned twenty out of the twenty-five traits listed:

1. For most of my life, I have avoided conflict and duck for cover when I hear sudden loud noises. In childhood, conflicts were not peaceably resolved, and loud noises meant bad things were likely to happen to me.

2. I have taught myself to gracefully accept compliments. In the past, I would deflect the compliment giver by returning one to him/her.

3. It was always my fault when I was growing up. Even now, I still blame myself too frequently.

4. I was an extreme apologizer for years, thanks to Jackie's rules. I've now learned to apologize when I have erred or hurt someone – and to make amends when appropriate.

5. I frequently stay at home as it's my safe haven. Some who know me feel I isolate myself there.

6. I trust until hurt, and then I close my emotional door.

7. With minor decisions, such as where to meet for lunch, I am indecisive. It's likely due to fear of the

likely repercussions from my choice being wrong while growing up.

8. I rarely say anything that someone else will disagree with. Instead, I'll listen and not state my opinion.

9. I protect myself both with the words I use and energetically. It's time for me to live and speak from my heart.

10. I respect most authority figures and always do what I believe is right. Getting into trouble with an authority figure would ignite one of my innermost fears.

11. I have learned not to explain myself with unnecessary detail.

12. Saying no is still very difficult for me.

13. I frequently find myself doing something someone else could so that I know it will be done correctly. I'd rather do it myself than ask for help.

14. It still takes courage for me to speak my emotional truths. Once again, it is because of the childhood fear of being told I'm wrong.

15. I have a shadow side, just like everyone else. I am learning to work with it as my teacher as I continue my self-improvement journey.

16. There are times I still believe I'm not good enough or smart enough. At least I'm much better at this than I once was.

17. It took years of work for me to make eye contact with people when speaking to them one-on-one. As with any endeavor, practice, practice, practice improves it.

18. I am still a novice at communicating my feelings, primarily because I am still learning how to identify them.

19. I'm not a fighter. I accept things as they are instead of being assertive. This is a cousin to "it's always my fault."

20. If something goes wrong, I know I am to blame because there is something I could have done better.

Overcoming emotional abuse provides me with frequent personal growth opportunities.

33

Too Painful to Sit Down

Since the first instance in 2003, there have been numerous occasions when the intense pain in my rectum made it far too painful to sit down. Walking around when it occurred usually allowed my mind to focus on something else.

I was able to reach Judy Goodman by phone the first time it happened. She removed the energy that had attacked my body and the horrific pain went away instantly.

To say that I was grateful is a great understatement, as the pain, dull and throbbing, was so intense it was all my mind could focus on at the time.

The root cause of the pain was the feeling of what it was like to be sodomized as a three-year-old. My body wasn't ready for, and certainly didn't want, a grown man's penis to penetrate my rectum.

In 2005, Uncle Clyde's health took a serious turn for the worse. He was living in a multi-story retirement home in Houston. I visited him many times while he was a resident there.

For a man who would rather be saltwater wade fishing than sleeping, moving into that small apartment must have been hard.

The Sunday before he died, I drove to Houston to see him, not knowing it would be my last trip to see him alive. He was comatose and had a lady watching over and taking care of him.

She let me stay with him for a few minutes and then I said my goodbyes. By the time I reached the elevator, I was attacked by the sharpest pain in the rectum I had ever felt to that point in time.

It was so intense I knew there was no way I could make the three-hour drive home. With blessed timing, I was able to reach Judy once again.

I related to her what had happened to me. She knew I was close to Uncle Clyde.

Then she asked me why I had made the trip to see him that day. My answer was the obvious one. I went to say my goodbyes, to let him know how much he'd meant to me in my life and how much I truly loved him.

Judy let me know that was the superficial reason I made the trek. I absolutely didn't get the unseen reason.

Then Judy shared that Uncle Clyde had been sexually assaulted as a child by men, just as I had been. He wasn't meant to carry that energy across the veil when he died, as it wasn't his burden.

What she said made sense then. Uncle Clyde absolutely despised having his picture taken. That was a certain sign of being sexually abused for me, which I had learned from Sara.

Judy removed the energy from me, and the pain that went with it. I was then able to drive myself home with ease, but with much to ponder regarding Uncle Clyde's childhood.

Many more times that pain would come to me out-of-the-blue, but usually less intense and I was able to remove it myself.

In 2015 a niece and her fiancé planned their wedding on the Turks and Caicos island of Providenciales. What a truly beautiful place it was!

I opted to stay at a motel up the beach from the hotel where everyone else attending the wedding was staying, as I wanted some time to myself for a break, instead of socializing.

The motel I stayed in had a wonderful beach, nice amenities, and restaurants that served delicious food. It was the right place for me.

Though the high temperature for the day only reached the mid-eighties, my time in the sun the day before was too much for my body. As I tan easily, in Texas an hour and a half at that temperature would barely darken my skin tone.

Not so on that island. My ankles were badly sun-burned and swollen for the first time in my life.

I opted to have an early lunch and return to my room to take a long nap.

On the way back to my room on the third floor, I saw a maintenance man a short distance away and instinctively knew to stay away from him. He wasn't a bad man, but there was something in his energy field I wanted to avoid.

Instead of walking up the outside stairs to my third-floor room I decided to take the elevator. As it was on the way down to pick me up, I happened to glance to my right.

The maintenance man turned the corner and walked right past me, beginning his trip up the stairs. Immediately the most intense pain I had ever felt as an adult hit my rectum. It was more intense than what I had felt from Uncle Clyde.

Somehow, I made it to my room. All I could do was lie down and hope.

Once prone, I said prayers, pleading to Mother/Father God for relief from the pain I felt...

Nothing happened.

Before I decided to cry myself to sleep (hopefully), I asked for help. Many times since I awakened in 1998, unique hand positions would come to me unexpectedly.

I asked to be shown the hand position to relieve the rectal pain I felt from being sodomized. Within a matter of seconds, I was given two hand positions.

One was for a man who had been sodomized and the other for women who had been raped.

As soon as the fingers on my right and left hands hit the right spot on the opposite hand the pain went away for good. Then I was able to relax and soon afterward take the nap my body desired.

As intense as the rectal pain was for me to bear, I thanked the maintenance man for walking past me. I truly hope I cleared away the pain he was carrying with him too, if for his highest and best good.

Next, I thanked my guides, angels and ascended masters on the other side of the veil as well as Mother/Father God. It was because of them I was able to find those special hand positions.

With the hand positions in tow, now when that energy hits me I am able to clear it away in a matter of seconds. It is a pain no one should ever have to feel or remember.

Again, I am extremely grateful for the many blessings I enjoy in this life. Being able to sit down pain-free is one of them.

34

No Longer Do I Have Problems

In the mid-1990's, Jean Mollard, a community visionary, invited me to have breakfast with her at the Hamburger Bar in Palestine. It's a '50s style diner that has a very rustic but authentic interior.

They served the best breakfasts in town, still do, and have good southern home cooked meals for lunches plus the best onion rings in town, too!

I took my daughters, Susanna, Frances and Lucy there many times when they were growing up. The recipes and the wait staff are still the same.

Betty, their longtime server, remembers my daughters' names whenever they come in for a return visit. The place remains a favorite for my girls.

That morning Jean had a community project to discuss with me. She was on a Texas Parks and Wildlife advisory committee. During her tenure there, she met Ken, a gentleman from the Texas A&M Extension Service home office.

Jean told me about the Texas Parks & Wildlife Department's commitment to help communities build parks, with a $500,000 grant funded by revenue derived from the Texas cigarette tax.

Communities which applied for the park grant had to fill out an application, which would be scored based on their selective criteria. Only the best one was selected each year.

Each applicant community had to come up with matching funds. They could be either cash or a cash equivalent such as donated services.

Jean asked my thoughts about getting a group of community leaders together to take a bus tour of parks in South Central and Southeast Texas. I thought the idea was stellar.

Anything Jean does is always well planned and carried out with excellence!

Within a couple of months, a group of volunteers gathered for the community spirit team bus tour. It came at a good time, as there was a division in our community once again. For each generation, it seems there's always someone in the community who is miserable. They take out their personal feelings on others to make themselves feel better and delight in the attention they receive from those who also want to complain. Whether it was W. E. Barrow back in my dad's time on city council, or Joe Ed Bunton when I served as mayor, they complain loudly and rarely, if ever, offered solutions.

Ken and Larry Womack, who was the then district manager for Texas Power & Light Company, agreed to serve as co-facilitators. Together they were a dynamic and magical force for us.

They put us in small groups while on the bus and threw problems at us to solve. Each group session led to developing togetherness in our community, which was sorely lacking at the time.

After a lengthy drive, we arrived in communities such as Baytown and Port Aransas, Texas. We were given tours of the parks those communities had built with the Texas Parks and Wildlife Department's Grant Funds. Community leaders met with us and we discovered that each community's resources and methodology was different.

Ken let us know that every successful community applicant had difficulties to overcome. I'll always remember how he described them.

His premise was that communities don't have problems, they have opportunities, instead. I latched onto his idea.

Our community volunteers and the co-facilitators were on the bus tour for roughly thirty-six hours. Nine of it was for sleep and breakfast the next morning. Everyone on the bus came back invigorated. We were excited and full of energy for our community endeavors.

In those days our town had no soccer fields, so it was decided that was the community need for us to tackle. Jean helped supervise the project, with much help from Steve Presley and numerous other folks.

We won, and proudly built Stephen Bennett Park with four soccer fields and some nature features as well. (Captain Stephen Bennett was a community resident who was killed in combat during the Vietnam War.)

I took Ken's quote to heart and applied it to people too. I never call something I'm facing a problem, because if I call it a problem, then with certainty it becomes one.

By referring to it as an opportunity, it becomes just that.

Opportunities abound in my life just as they do in yours. It's how I perceive them that has made the greatest difference.

**"No longer do I have problems.
I merely have opportunities instead."**

Jackson Hanks

35

Are You Running?

"We can evade reality, but we cannot evade
the consequences of evading reality."

Ayn Rand

"The truth that many people never understand,
until it is too late, is that the more you try to
avoid suffering the more you suffer, because
smaller and more insignificant things begin to
torture you in proportion to your fear of being
hurt."

Thomas Merton

With a very deep sigh, I confess that for years in my life I was a "running from myself" track star. In fact, I may have been the champion of them all. In truth, at the time I had no clue, no idea that I was running, or that the extra time at work and beer consumption was my way of doing that.

Just another hour at work (being responsible,
you know); a beer; a cigarette; just one more

joint; a glass of wine; going online to find the love you are missing (and deserving); placing a bet; going to another ball game; emotional eating; spending Saturday morning at the office; going out with the guys for a beer/drink/ pool game; a business trip disguised; a sexual liaison; picking a fight over something trivial, or eating certain foods you know are not good for you.

As a lawyer, it is important to "get it right."

A primary area of my law practice is real estate law. The rules in Texas are picky, so years ago I thought I was being super responsible because I was spending more and more time at the office. I'd arrive by 6:30 am and might not leave until 6 pm.

I was super busy. It was important, or so I thought.

I was already spending Saturday mornings at the office then. When my kiddos began attending services at an out-of-town church, spending Sunday mornings at the office became fair game too.

Accomplishing my work on time afforded me the opportunity to spend time on my civic volunteer endeavors. Yes, I was always there for my children and their activities, both scholastic and extracurricular ones.

By the time I stacked more on my plate financially, business-wise and as an elected official, the toxicity of what I had to deal with regarding the latter led me to begin relying on a solution that in truth was just the opposite - an avoidance.

I buried my emotional pain each day by masking it with Miller Lite beer, beginning in earnest the day the vicious rumor began circulating about me while I was serving as mayor.

Instead of being super responsible after work and on Sundays, I began zoning out as my solution. I started watching Western movies at home on late Sunday mornings. Unfortunately, what my emotional self demanded as its elixir did not solve any of the crises I faced.

To my eternal gratitude, several years later, due to an angelic/spiritual visit, my life forever changed.

Through a simple human hug in public, I surrendered the beer "god" I had daily worshipped. Overnight, I went from consuming around seventy or more cans of beer a week to zero, with no meds, meetings or withdrawals.

Miraculously, I just stopped. The chemical dependency was taken from me.

The miracle hug happened on the outdoor patio of the café serving food and beverages at Tyler Pounds Field Airport. It happened lawyer-to-lawyer.

I had made arrangements with the other lawyer's administrative assistant to pick her up at the airport, and to later return her there for her flight back to Houston. Making that arrangement, to me, was the gentlemanly thing to do.

The lady lawyer was a presenter at a conference on title insurance matters. My title company (Texas First Title Company, LLC) had become a recently licensed title agency by the Texas Department of Insurance.

Though I was (and continue to be) a board-certified lawyer in both Residential as well as Farm & Ranch Real Estate Law, the maze of procedural and rate rules of Texas title insurance are amazingly complex. They were difficult for me to understand at first. Twenty years later, I'm still learning something new every day!

Another lawyer presenter arrived early afternoon and we chatted in the restaurant as they ate a late lunch.

After the conference ended, I dutifully returned the lady lawyer presenter to the airport. We had a great chat on matters spiritual on the way.

I felt it my gentlemanly duty to stay with her for a bit as her return flight to Houston was a couple of hours from departure. Our chat, during that time, was just East Texas fun and laughter. She had a great wit and used it well.

My inner clock chimed when it was time for me to return to Palestine. That clock has put me in places and times that have amazed me many times in my life. I had met the lady lawyer at a large conference previously, where we shook hands after making the acquaintance. She does have a firm grip (strong handshake), as we say in Texas. This time I decided to be brave and give her a hug. Mind you, the hug was in public.

It felt like it lasted five minutes, but in reality, it lasted about two seconds. I stepped back from the hug and was utterly speechless.

Being in that state is highly uncommon for any lawyer, myself included.

I finally managed to get words to come out of my mouth - and were they ever profound!

"I'm sorry, I don't know what to say," was all I could manage.

Using my manners, I courteously excused myself, but was in some kind of an altered state of mind. Reaching my car, I turned off the radio, which was extremely unusual for me then.

While driving from Tyler to Palestine I was in some sort of a fog which I had never experienced before, nor have since.

When I arrived home, my family had already left to attend a Friday night high school soccer game. I just missed them.

Normally, I would have consumed more beer that evening than most men would consume in a month. However, that evening was different.

I drank one beer, went to the soccer game and stayed until half-time. Returning home, I drank one more beer, then went straight to bed at what was a very early hour for me.

The next day, even when the daily cravings for a beer usually kicked in, I had the opposite of desiring to have one. I really, really didn't want one. A miracle in my life had removed the chemical dependency from my false support system.

I had instantly shifted from running from my feelings into having physical body and emotional memories showing up out of nowhere, including the feelings I had buried for much of my lifetime. Now sober, I also discovered the reasons I had spent as much time at the office as I did, and why the next beer was so important.

In truth, I was in avoidance of the feelings I had buried way down inside me from childhood: not good enough, can't get it right, no self-worth, and wanting to be respected like my dad. My dad was adored by many in my hometown, as they had no idea of the terrible violence he and Jackie had inflicted on me during my childhood.

Later, post-divorce, I just knew I could get it right by meeting the right woman. I gave it my best, but in retrospect, I have to laugh at my past with tears streaming. That path I took was absolutely the worst way to heal from my inner wounds.

In pursuit of Ms. Right, I did meet several exceptional and truly wonderful ladies, each of whom helped me become a better person. They did so by encouraging me to get in touch with my feelings, which up to that point had been ignored.

It was when I started digging into my child within (inner child) work that I began figuring out the solution. I had avoided this work for many years.

Post-divorce I discovered a very humbling secret about relationships, especially my relationship with myself.

Until I learned to love myself just as I was, where I was, without any sort of stimulant or company, I was running from the unlearned emotional lessons of my past.

I finally stopped running from those that had been chasing me. As I have learned, and forgive me for repeating myself but this has been so important for me - when missed, lessons change places, faces and times, but always increase in intensity until they are learned.

If we fail to learn them in time, the energy of the lesson missed becomes our "dis-ease" which, if then ignored, can become the reason we die.

We all avoid things, and people, in our lives. It is called escape. Yet in truth, there is no such thing as an escape in our life's one act play.

The choice is ours. Run and die, or stop, re-mold ourselves and live!

I stopped and remolded my life - and that made an amazing difference!

36

The Weight of Words

In 2012, I began working with the concept of the weight of words. Whether positive or negative, our words and thoughts have tremendous impacts on our lives.

I remember some of Jackie's favorite words spoken to me in childhood were, "Shame on you," "I'll shoot your feet off," and "How dare you?"

Shaming me was her chosen method of child-rearing.

As a result of the way I was raised, I often find fault with myself before anyone can say a word. Reading Darlene Lancer's book, *Codependency for Dummies*, helped me understand how my learned, self-fault-finding isn't normal or emotionally healthy.

My friend, Paula Reed, taught me that when a sentence begins with "If, And, Why, But or You," you will likely shame the person you are speaking to, or you will feel shamed if you are on the receiving end of such sentences. I have found there is truth to her wisdom.

We are steeped in cultural negativity. Political pundits shame us for not thinking and believing their toxic brew. In print, by voice and as acted by others on television, we're bombarded with messages letting us know we're not good enough – because we don't own or use their products.

I discerned something special back in 2012. Out-of-nowhere, I figured out where words and thoughts land on our bodies and why.

Each of us has an invisible "meridian" that exists in our bodies. It runs at the base of our lungs and goes from one side of the body to the other.

When shaming or other negative words are spoken they land on our body below that invisible line. The same thing is true for those types of words we speak to others. Our words land below the line on the person we are speaking to.

Positive words spoken by and to us do the exact same thing as their negative cousins. The only difference is that they land above the invisible line.

Often we say to ourselves and tell others what it is we don't want in life. Yet focusing on what we don't want assures we'll receive more of that - exactly what we don't want.

It took me a spell to figure this out, but here goes. In the past, when I wanted to encourage someone and uplift them, I'd say, "Beyond a shadow of a doubt, Lisa, today is going to be a great day for you!"

What I didn't know or realize back then is that I had just doomed Lisa's day. I did so by planting a seed of doubt in her mind - the total opposite of my intention!

It took time, but I came up with how to phrase my intention properly. It's super easy, I said, "Lisa, with absolute certainty, today is going to be a great day for you!"

That sentence told Lisa my truth. I encourage you to practice feeling where your words and thoughts land. The quoted sentences are good examples to start with.

Words powerfully imprint us, and others too. When I say at the office, "Rhonda, don't forget to take the trash out," I have created a result that's certain to happen, though not my intent.

It's not whether Rhonda will forget to take the trash out. Instead it's only a question of time. Like it or not, Rhonda will someday forget to take out the trash, thanks to her being imprinted.

As taking the trash out in a timely fashion is my desire, it's important for me to change my words. I do so by saying, "Rhonda, please remember to take the trash out."

That way, I imprint her to remember instead of to forget. As with the first two example sentences, practice feeling where the sentences land. They either land above or below the line. A few can be neutral and land directly on the line.

When I hear words spoken to me, or by me, land above the magical line, they are positive and encouraging. We all like those words!

Words that land below the invisible line are heavy. They impact us and stay there until we deal with them and their root cause.

For several years, I taught the Leadership Palestine Class about the power of words. It is put on by the Palestine Area Chamber of Commerce, whose executive director told me each year that it was one of the participants' favorite classes. One of the reasons why is that I taught them in an experiential way.

Mind you, there are years in which I followed Jean Mollard as a class presenter. She is an amazing speaker, who is chock-full of facts and positive words for her class.

She is a super tough act to follow because she's fantastic at public speaking.

Here is a fabulous quote. To me it is absolute truth:

"I've learned that people will forget what you said, people will forget what you did, but people will never forget how you made them feel."

Maya Angelou

I muse and tell folks that every community has a radio station. It's located at 102.1 on the FM radio dial and its call letters are WBMC. (Of course, the station is fictitious.)

Think of all the people you know in your community, and in your life, who are card-carrying members of the "Whine, Bitch, Moan & Complain" (WBMC) fraternity or sorority.

**Complaints have never produced
one solution in my life!**

When faced with a negative situation, I've learned to use these words with folks, "Help me understand..." It's always important to me that I discern what the underlying cause is.

All of the folks who smashed the proverbial door in my face that you read about in this book were my teachers. Sure, my nose bled and bloodied my face, but they presented lessons and opportunities for me to learn.

The more I learn from the door being slammed in my face the better off I am. It gives me a chance to ward off the same experience at a later date. It's called "learning the lesson."

It took a couple of years for me to shift the words I speak to the positive channel. People likely thought I was a dolt back then, as I would listen and pause. The pause I took before verbalizing my reply allowed me a gift. I was able to change any negative words or phrases to their positive counterpart.

Being positive in my thoughts and words blesses me in more ways than my conscious mind can fathom.

37

Earaches

As an adult, when our girls were pre-school aged I looked forward to going home after work. I would get them to join me in the backyard where I would swing them on the swing set.

After a spell, the magic of the swing set was lost, and I would call on my inner elf and make up fun games for them to play. One was to see if they could knock their daddy down.

Of course, to be certain they were safe, I'd only pretend to be knocked backwards until they were older, but the effect was the same each time. They'd laugh, chortle and giggle whenever they saw their daddy flailing his arms and stumbling backwards as if they had stunned me with their little feet and legs.

There were other silly, playful games we played as well. It was a magical time for each one of us.

Looking back to my own childhood, there simply was no comparison. There were frequent arguments that never led to a pleasant ending. When alcohol was involved, what happened was worse for me as a child.

I didn't like such conflict and tried to avoid being seen or heard when it happened. In the small house we lived in when I was a child, there was no such thing as escaping.

Sometimes after such conflict, an earache would settle into one of my ears. I was taken to the doctor numerous times due to my throbbing ear aches, which were often accompanied by fever in my body. Most times eardrops were prescribed, and they had to be warmed on the stove.

The drops, plus sticking a wad of cotton in my ear, usually helped them dissipate and finally leave my body after a few days.

I wasn't consciously trying to avoid school - or life itself, but my subconscious mind knew better, as the little boy body I inhabited really needed a break. My body usually took two to three days to recover from having those painful earaches. When accompanied by a sore throat, add on a few more days.

It wasn't until the third grade that the doctor recommended that my tonsils be removed. Surgery back in 1960 was far different than it is today!

After the doctor removed my tonsils, my childhood earaches left for good.

As written by Dr. Lincoln, Ph.D. (1991, 4th Rev. 2006, p. 200) it's no wonder I was besieged by earaches early in childhood. In his book *Messages From the Body,* he describes "hearing-fearing." What they are hearing is causing them great inner pain. They feel they are surrounded by internal and/or external discord and conflict and they are "fed up to their ears" with it all.

"They feel accountable for the conflict and responsible for its resolution, but they feel unable to do anything about it, and so they are now hyper-sensitive to conflict and turmoil. It reminds them too much of their parents arguing and the absence of peace, harmony and love in their family."

Michael J. Lincoln, Ph.D.

Dr. Lincoln's words hit home with me. My growing up home was loaded with toxicity.

38

I Am Responsible For Me

I was raised by stern parents to always do what is right. I quickly learned the painful consequences by being spanked hard or hit upside the head or shoulders when I didn't do so.

Given the childhood memories I've mined, my greatest self-surprise is that I have learned to feel the life force energy of thoughts, words and actions, both my own and from others.

It didn't come fast or easy for me though. In the energy wellness courses I took prior to starting the child within work, I was amazed at the subtle energies which many women and a few men felt.

I didn't feel a thing. That's because my figurative emotional onion was perfectly intact, outer skin and all, including its roots.

In order to begin feeling life force energies at all, I had to do a good deal of child within work with Sara over an intense two-year period. After that, there was something even more important required of me.

I had to become vulnerable and open myself up to feeling the subtle sensations life force has.

A friend took me to a rock, gem and mineral show in Dallas, with many vendors with all sorts of interesting looking rocks. I found two that I liked and proudly took them home.

The next morning, in my quiet time, I held a quartz crystal in my right hand. With my eyes closed, I felt its energy.

I put it down thinking I had just made something up. To test myself, I picked up the quartz crystal again and felt the same thing.

It felt stronger in my right hand than in my left. At last I had opened myself up to feeling life force energies. Often times, they are subtle.

Much has changed in the environment we live in since then, and I believe it is much easier now to feel those energies than it was when I first started.

As humans our range of what we can see with our eyes and hear with our ears is a small fraction of those spectrums. I read an article that estimated that the visible light our eyes see in the electromagnetic spectrum comprises only two percent or less of it. The normal range of sounds humans can hear is between 20 hertz (Hz) and 20,000 Hz. Dolphins' hearing range, on the other hand, is between 1000 Hz and 150,000 Hz.

I am the one who had to do the work in order to open myself up to feeling life force energies. No one could do the work for me.

It was the same when Sara told me to start reading Terrence Real's book, *I Don't' Want to Talk About it: Overcoming the Secret Legacy of Male Depression*. My assignment was a chapter a night.

In my next session with Sara, I told her that his book was very difficult for me to read as it was filled with lots of psychological words and concepts that were new to me.

Sara then asked if I could read a page a day. I promised that I would.

Within a couple of weeks, I was able to read up to five pages a night. Two Sara sessions later, I let her know that I was now reading a chapter a day.

What Sara gave me was a success tool to work with. Her understanding of why his book was a challenge for me helped enormously. Her success formula worked even better as she commended me for sticking with the book and reading what I could each night.

Though it was a hard read, I confess I was in the group for whom he wrote the book. I am a man who didn't have a clue why his work was so important.

I learned that I had the all the traits of a man hiding his depression.

I didn't believe my office hours were wasted time.

For me, it took every one of them to earn enough money to support my family. Yet I acknowledged Terrence's accuracy. I had been depressed and had masked the symptoms.

It would have been super uncomfortable for me to talk about them. Back then, though, I didn't even know why I worked Saturday and Sunday mornings too.

As you've read, it was years later when I learned the power and feeling of my thoughts and words and worked to improve them. I'm human, and there are days I slip a bit with them, especially in traffic!

I have begun reminding myself when that happens to say out loud, "Wow, and thank you, God!" Doing so takes me out of my ego's desires and gives me a chance to recognize two things.

One, when in a hurry, we often meet resistance. That's just the Universe's way of staying in balance.

Secondly, it allows me to realize I'm only in charge of and responsible for myself. I'm not responsible for you or anyone else.

As I learned in Al-Anon, my job is to keep my side of the street clean. That means I am responsible for cleaning up all messes I make, though when appropriate I am glad to help others. It is not my responsibility to point out their mistakes, foibles or messes unless they are directed at me personally.

Keeping my side of the proverbial street clean is a daily exercise. And it is a very important one for me.

That's because whatever I give to someone else carries emotional stuff from inside me that is invisible to most human eyes. Those who have what I call the gift of sight, or otherwise known as clairvoyants, see that stuff just as you and I see birds in flight.

I apologize when I've done something wrong. Then I make amends, if appropriate. Making amends means that I have to change parts of my emotional self so I don't make the same mistake again.

> **Though I work with gifted professionals,**
> **it is up to me to incorporate their work**
> **to make lasting changes within myself.**
> **I am responsible for me.**
> **No one else on planet Earth is.**

I choose to continue my self-improvement and inner growth.

My desire is to become the best person I can be. I still have room for improvement!

Whatever I carry inside me impacts others by my thoughts, words and actions. That includes emotional junk that is stirred up, as well as emotional treasures I may feel at the time.

> **I am responsible for me and that includes my**
> **thoughts, words and actions towards others.**
> **It also includes my physical, mental and**
> **emotional health.**

39

God Loves Me – Just As I Am

Several years ago, I attended a seminar in Denver, Colorado. Thanks to my childhood experiences, I've always been observant.

For some reason, I saw many cars with bumper stickers. Some had clever sayings and some had a bit of wisdom.

One bumper sticker hit me deep in my heart. It read, "God Loves Me Just as I Am."

If other folk had not been nearby I would have dropped to one knee and cried. Instead, I sucked up my emotional desire and held onto it until a later time.

The saddest part of my life, to me, is that I call upon and have a closer relationship with God when life is hard. That's true whether given physical challenges or emotional ones.

During the early part of my child within recovery work, I was close to Mother God daily. The memories were horrific and repulsive to me.

Though what happened to me is truth, there were times I just wanted to go "home" (or as many would say "heaven"). I wasn't suicidal, it was more that the load I carried was almost more than I could bear.

The tears I shed back then came from deep within me, having been held onto for way too long. I consider it a gift and blessing that I was given the chance to remember my childhood past and to work through as many of the experiences as I have.

I've helped raise three wonderful daughters. Thanks be to God that somehow I managed to break the cycles of abuse I experienced, though I was not aware of being abused as a child until 1999.

Am I a perfect dad? Absolutely not.

I did my best to raise them in a way that by the time they were ready to leave their parents' nest, they had strong wings to carry them and good values to guide them.

I wasn't a perfect dad and of course I know there are things I could have done to better help my girls. I did my best, but there certainly was room for improvement by me.

In business, as a lawyer, elected official, friend, husband, companion, member of non-profit organizations and in all other aspects of my life, I own my mistakes and failures. I deeply regret each one.

As you have likely surmised through this book, thanks to my childhood, I'm very hard on myself. If I make a mistake, I usually own it before someone else points it out to me. That is just another sad trait I have to do some work on to overcome my codependent traits.

It is from failures and hard knocks in life that I have grown the most emotionally, as an adult. Had I not experienced the horrific events that I did in childhood, I would not have worked with the extraordinary professionals mentioned in this book. Nor would I be the person I am today.

Through it all, God was always with me and loves me just as I am, just as God loves you, just as you are.

Though God loves me just as I am, I am still responsible for my thoughts, words and actions. I choose to meet the consequences of all of them head on.

40

Texas Road Hand

Early on during my tenure as mayor of Palestine, Bobby Evans, the Texas Department of Transportation (TxDoT) District Engineer, whose office was in Tyler, Texas, reached out to me.

He was looking for someone in our county who shared his vision of an improved road system for our residents. I was more than glad to be that person, and let him know so.

From what I have been told, Bobby is a legend within TxDoT. He treats all people as he would like to be treated, has excellent communication skills, is the top in his field regarding proper engineering of roads and bridges, is a team builder and leads by example.

I consider it a gift and a privilege that Bobby reached out to me. At the time, our county had numerous important highways that were only two-lane roads. Palestine is a central hub, where U.S. Highways 79, 84 and 287 converge, as do Texas State Highways 19 and 155.

Though the rights-of-way had been acquired to widen those roads, as well as to build the North Loop 256 around Palestine, no construction funding had been pursued or received in years for such projects. Fortunately though, Palestine's South Loop had been built in the late 1960s.

Our first big success came when Bobby told me he had found the money to construct Palestine's North Loop. I believe that was in 1990. The town's city council had to approve the construction as it involved moving some local utilities.

I found it hard to fathom, but Joe Ed Bunton and his buddy on council, Dr. R. E. Weardon, a chiropractor, fought it with all they could manage. Criticism came easy for both of them, but change not so much.

When the time came for the council vote I was very concerned. Losing this opportunity could kill any other highway projects that might come our town's way for years to come.

Fortunately, when the votes were cast, a majority approved, regardless of loud dissent from Joe Ed and Dr. Weardon. The approval set off a chain of events, at least in my mind, that finally brought Palestine forward in time to having an excellent road transportation system, though such didn't occur until well after I was mayor.

From the late 1980s through the mid-1990s, our local chamber of commerce arranged several trips to Austin to appear before the TxDoT Commissioners, as they had a strong say as to which significant road improvements in each district would be approved for funding.

Once the North Loop 256 project was approved, Bobby had community leaders, including the county judge, submit paperwork to TxDoT.

Whoever is in charge of approving the Texas Road Hand Award recipients deemed it proper that I was to be given such award. I was completely stunned when I was presented with the 126th Texas Road Hand Award at a community luncheon before the North Loop 256 project started construction. To say I'm both honored and humbled to have received the award is a great understatement.

Though, as written elsewhere in this book, receiving awards is not what motivates me to do things to help improve whatever it is I can. Seeing the need, finding the solution(s) and teaching by example are what motivate me.

Completion of the North Loop project in Palestine made it significantly easier for the traveling public, especially eighteen-wheeler truckers, to skip the congestion and lights on the South Loop. Its completion initiated a relief valve that over-the-road haulers vastly prefer to use.

By 2001 or so, our community had the opportunity to send representatives to appear before the TxDoT Commissioners in Austin, Texas, at their monthly meeting regarding the proposed widening of State Highway 155 from Palestine to Tyler. Not only was it a two-lane road, it had numerous hills and much truck traffic on the road.

You could almost always count on it being a slow ride for part of the way. Sometimes it was both slow and dangerous.

The late Hon. Bascom Bentley was selected as one of our presenters. Bascom had the gift of the gab and was personal friends with one of the Highway Commissioners, Rick Williamson.

Though we were scheduled to present long before 11:00 a.m., the buzzer and red light in my head sounded. I knew I had to leave as I had an appointment that day to see Sara Hays at 2:00 p.m.

I bid adieu to the community group of supporters for the project and truly wished I could have stayed to see Bascom make his presentation. Later, I found out that he not only presented our case, he put on a performance no one at TxDoT had ever witnessed before during one of those solemn meetings. Only Bascom could pull something like that off and get away with it, for everyone was laughing to tears from what I was told.

The TxDoT Commissioners approved the State Highway 155 widening project. Approval never means construction, it's just the next step in the process, so I was relieved when construction contracts were let and construction began soon thereafter.

Now Texas State Highway 155 is a four-lane divided highway. It makes the drive between Palestine, Tyler and other connecting cities from there easy.

Lastly, just a few months prior to this book's publication, the widening project for U. S. 79, from inside the city limits of Palestine westward to the Trinity River, was completed. The Trinity River is the western boundary of Anderson County, Texas, of which Palestine is its county seat.

Soon after I had received the Road Hand Award, Steve Presley asked me what it took to be recognized as such. I let him know my formula, which included being a partner with the district engineer and resident engineers in our district. It also entailed going to as many meetings as possible to support them, as what they propose almost always benefits the community at large, though there are always the nay-sayers.

When I was mayor, I did everything within my power to support Bobby Evans' mission for us. In my opinion, he did more to improve our road transportation system than any other district engineer did in my lifetime.

Steve then became elected to the town's city council in 2006 and served his district admirably for many years. He now serves as our mayor and truly wants to see the town become the best it can be.

In 2013, Steve attended a statewide TxDoT meeting in Tyler, Texas that was supported by video cameras in each district engineer's office. Steve gave up attending a campaign fundraising event for a popular state senator in order to attend. Joining Steve was the Director of Public Works for the city, as well as others from the District Engineers' office.

During the meeting the statewide TxDoT district participants were invited to discuss projects that were "shovel-ready." That means all preliminary work has been done, including all environmental studies, design work and right-of-way acquisitions.

Very few other districts had one, so Steve was delighted to tell them about our transportation need and that yes, indeed we had a "shovel-ready" project.

The project was approved because President Obama had found monies available through the Federal Highway Administration that would help stimulate the national economy with infrastructure (road) improvements.

Thanks be to all who have helped make road improvements possible in our community. Special thanks, though, go to Steve Presley.

It was his special efforts that helped eliminate an enormous traffic bottleneck west of town. As a result of his following the formula I used when mayor, our community benefitted from receiving a $40 million construction project from TxDoT.

It was a project that had been on the board for years. We'd even been teased a time or two that it was going to be approved, then suddenly TxDoT would run out of money.

Once the project was approved by TxDoT, I was more than pleased to nominate Steve for the Texas Road Hand Award. He truly deserved it, and was honored by TxDoT officials at a community luncheon in Palestine in 2016 as the 242nd Texas Road Hand recipient.

There is great power in leading by example.

41

Walmart 6036 Facility

I was elected mayor of Palestine, Texas, in May, 1989. Time passed quickly, but progress was slow due to community divisiveness.

In early spring 1990, I received a call at my law office from a Mr. Smith from Walmart's corporate office in Bentonville, Arkansas.

In no uncertain terms, Mr. Smith let me know that their Distribution Center #6005, located inside the city limits of Palestine, had the highest workers' compensation and ad valorem taxation costs in their distribution chain, and that this was not acceptable.

He asked me what the city could do. I didn't have the answer for him, but promised I would call him back as soon as I could give him effective resolutions for their issues.

I knew that we had several hundred jobs at stake. When I took the reigns as mayor, our town had just experienced what a horrific bust in the oil field brought to us. Many good paying jobs were lost, and a fair number of commercial buildings became vacant.

It was imperative that our community save the Walmart jobs.

In those days, the only training available to learn how to become an effective mayor was on the job training. Using your wisdom and intuition helped too, though.

For a few years prior to my serving as mayor, my wife and I subscribed to both the local newspaper, *Palestine Herald Press,* and to the Tyler, Texas newspaper, *Tyler Morning Telegraph.* After receiving Mr. Smith's call, I remembered that Tyler had hired Tom Mullins to be the President/CEO of the Tyler Economic Development Council in June of 1989.

Since then, Tom was selected as the President/CEO of the Tyler Chamber of Commerce too. Tom's accomplishments in the Tyler area are truly remarkable and he is regarded as an economic development/chamber guru throughout the State of Texas now.

That he has served in those capacities for this length of time is a testament to the incredible job Tom has done for Tyler, Texas.

As I had no knowledge of economic development tools or incentives available in Texas, I instinctively knew that my first action was to reach out to Tom Mullins. He was cordial on the phone and asked how he could help.

I related Mr. Smith's call and explained my ignorance about possible solutions. Tom asked if we had an Enterprise Zone and other economic development tools in place. My response to Tom was, "What are those?"

Tom's view of economic development back in those days was refreshing to me. His vision was that if a community outside Tyler benefitted from doing well, Tyler would receive its fair share of economic activity from those outlying communities.

He was absolutely right, as Tyler was and remains the largest community in East Texas. Shoppers tend to shop in locales that have things they can't buy locally. Palestine residents have shopped, dined, purchased vehicles and used Tyler's doctors and medical facilities for years.

Once Tom let me know what the available incentives were in Texas, I understood how far behind the curve our town was in that category. We had a lot of ground to cover quickly, if possible.

After Tom told me what to do and how to go about it, I called Mr. Smith to inform him of the tools I had learned about. I also let him know that time was of the essence for us, and that I'd do my best to get the incentives approved as quickly as possible.

I began scheduling breakfast meetings with important city businessmen and elected officials from all the entities that would have to pass resolutions approving the economic development incentives Tom had suggested. Tom also sent his assistant, Eric Davis, to educate those attending the meetings.

Eric was both knowledgeable and convincing. Either Palestine stepped up to the plate by adding the incentives - or we could be stuck where we were. I added, "or worse off," as we had hundreds of jobs in jeopardy.

Fortunately, Tyler had adopted those incentives and they had already begun to bear fruit. Knowing that Tyler and other towns were way out in front of us helped awaken us all.

Although there was a lot of grumbling about losing out on every available tax dollar, nearly everyone who attended our weekly meetings came to the same conclusion. The elected bodies, which included Palestine's city council, Palestine ISD, Westwood ISD, the Anderson County Commissioner's Court and Trinity Valley Community College, all had to vote to approve the incentives.

My recollection is that within about two months our community's elected bodies all passed the requisite economic development incentive packages. There was much work to do in putting together our Enterprise Zone that involved governmental entities and elected officials.

Larry Womack, the new T. U. Electric District Manager, stepped up to the plate when he moved to town in 1992. He helped do what was necessary to bring the Enterprise Zone to fruition, and to have it approved by all governmental entities as well.

I heaved a huge sigh of relief once all elected entities, including Palestine's city council, passed the economic development incentives and Enterprise Zone. After all had passed their resolutions, I called to let Mr. Smith know.

Though as I recall, there was a polite, "Thank you," from Mr. Smith, I knew in my heart that our community had saved several hundred decent paying jobs.

However, unbeknownst to me at the time, there was something stirring in the backwaters at Walmart. I remember it was less than a year after the entities approved the incentive packages that Walmart announced their intention to build their Distribution Center #6036 near Tucker, a tiny community located a couple of miles from the western city limits of Palestine.

Once completed, it too employed several hundred folk, plus has a truck repair facility, and has had a significant economic impact on our town and county.

Thanks be to Tom Mullins for having the vision and reaching out to Palestine, a small community to its southwest. To this day, he remains a friend to us.

Having Walmart Distribution Center #6036 in our county is proof of one of my favorite sayings:

"I'd far rather be lucky than good!"

Jackson Hanks

Regardless of whether you call it luck, synchronicity, or a combination of determination and courage, I believe it took some of each for me to find all of the healing pieces in my life.

Without them all, I shudder to think of how my childhood past would be haunting me every day of my life.

I'd far rather be lucky than right, too!

42

Nosebleeds

As a young child, at times I had the chance to spend the night at Grandma Zula and Grandpa Dad's house. Grandma Zula was my dad's mom.

She had a circle of friends who hooked rugs for a hobby, and several family households boasted having one of Zula's rugs.

Her friends also enjoyed playing canasta, a fun card game that I was much too young to figure out how to play then, but was always allowed to watch.

Grandpa Dad was a banker whose favorite hobby was freshwater lake fishing. He was a kind, gentle man from what I remember. He died when I was only four years old.

As an adult, Uncle Clyde told me that numerous people who rode the passenger train from Palestine to Houston would find his office in the Cotton Exchange Building, located near the Missouri-Pacific passenger train station. He worked for Adams & Porter, a marine insurance agency.

Uncle Clyde told me that the folks who came to look him up thanked him from their hearts for what Grandpa Dad did to help them through their difficult times. If the bank he worked for in Palestine didn't make a loan, sometimes he managed to do so out of his own pocket.

Grandma Zula & Grandpa Dad's home was a safe place for me. Their maid, Katy, made the best pancakes I ever had. More important to me was that she was genuinely kind, gentle and cared about the well-being of those she worked for.

For Grandma Zula's part, she made quite a name for herself during World War II. She headed up the local USO (United Service Organization) chapter in Palestine. It was a stopover for war weary soldiers on leave.

From what I have been told by many, she assembled and managed a large group of women who helped provide those servicemen with Texas hospitality. Some would cook and bring hot food for the soldiers who had been dining on cold C-Rations (canned food) for months.

Though short of stature at less than five feet tall, I am told that Grandma Zula was a stern taskmaster and kept the ladies organized and in line.

With a safe place to spend the night, what happened on the many times I slept there made no sense to my grandparents, their maid, or me. During many of those nights my nose would bleed profusely.

I would awaken with matted hair, blood on my pajamas and, of course, on the pillow case. I'm so sorry that Katy had to clean up after me. Even now, I am self -sufficient and never want to make someone go out of their way to help me.

It wasn't until my recovery work with Sara that I remembered those nosebleed nights. I picked up Dr. Lincoln's book *Messages From The Body* to see what he had to say about nosebleeds. I was stunned by what I read.

Dr. Lincoln (1991, 4th Rev. 2006, p. 435) wrote "Blown Away," where he explained that children who were "suffering from some severe emotional shock, on the unconscious level, from what they saw... or experienced," can be jolted by new information.

Which in my case was finding myself in a safe and loving environment.

What really hit home for me were these words, "It has resurfaced an underlying chronic issue for them - which is their worthlessness feelings. They were, in effect, largely emotionally ignored as a child."

My emotional needs were largely ignored as a child.

That piece fit perfectly with the feelings of self-worthlessness I worked through in my recovery work. Recovering my feelings of self-worth was one of the most challenging topics in my years of digging out of my emotional cellar.

After I hit bottom and began working my way out of being truly "self-worthless," I came across a poem, *The Invitation,* written by Oriah "Mountain Dreamer" House. I have copied it here, with permission:

The Invitation by Oriah

It doesn't interest me
what you do for a living.
I want to know
what you ache for
and if you dare to dream
of meeting your heart's longing.

It doesn't interest me
how old you are.
I want to know
if you will risk
looking like a fool
for love

for your dream
for the adventure of being alive.

It doesn't interest me
what planets are
squaring your moon...
I want to know
if you have touched
the centre of your own sorrow
if you have been opened
by life's betrayals
or have become shrivelled and closed
from fear of further pain.

I want to know
if you can sit with pain
mine or your own
without moving to hide it
or fade it
or fix it.

I want to know
if you can be with joy
mine or your own
if you can dance with wildness
and let the ecstasy fill you
to the tips of your fingers and toes
without cautioning us
to be careful
to be realistic
to remember the limitations
of being human.

It doesn't interest me
if the story you are telling me

is true.
I want to know if you can
disappoint another
to be true to yourself.
If you can bear
the accusation of betrayal
and not betray your own soul.
If you can be faithless
and therefore trustworthy.

I want to know if you can see Beauty
even when it is not pretty
every day.
And if you can source your own life
from its presence.
I want to know
if you can live with failure
yours and mine
and still stand at the edge of the lake
and shout to the silver of the full moon,
"Yes."

It doesn't interest me
to know where you live
or how much money you have.
I want to know if you can get up
after the night of grief and despair
weary and bruised to the bone
and do what needs to be done
to feed the children.

It doesn't interest me
who you know
or how you came to be here.
I want to know if you will stand

in the centre of the fire
with me
and not shrink back.

It doesn't interest me
where or what or with whom
you have studied.
I want to know
what sustains you
from the inside
when all else falls away.

I want to know
if you can be alone
with yourself
and if you truly like
the company you keep
in the empty moments.

By Oriah "Mountain Dreamer" House
from her book, *The Invitation* ©
1999. Published by HarperONE, San
Francisco.

There were countless times during my long, self-worth
recovery process when I would take a few minutes to reread
the poem. Each time I did it gave me a bit of hope which
helped me make it through the rest of the day.

43

How Could Anyone?

The year 1999 was a year of drastic changes for me. I filed for divorce.

There wasn't any one thing which caused my action. It had taken years, but it finally came to me that I had to be out of my marriage and alone in order to overcome my childhood trauma.

For at least a year before, whenever I went into a book store some book would all but fall into my hands. Each of them helped opened my eyes, heart and mind as to what for me is now real.

As I went through the divorce process, my safe port was at Uncle Clyde's and Aunt Howard's home in Houston. I went there on many weekends to be out of town. Most of my friends were married, and during the divorce process I learned that it is a couple's world.

And then it happened.

One Friday afternoon, within a month of filing for divorce, as I was driving to Houston and was somewhere between my hometown of Palestine and Crockett, Texas, I felt a blow to my right shoulder, close to my neck. It smarted so mightily that I cringed from it.

I was alone in the car.

Soon I felt another hard smack. This time the target was my head. It was a stunning blow, too.

The smacks continued for about fifteen minutes. I kept the information to myself and filed it away, thinking it was just some random event coming out of nowhere.

Instead of being a one-time occurrence, the breath-stopping blows continued every few days for a spell. They only happened when I was alone and quiet.

It took me a month or so to go far enough back into my childhood to fetch some memories. I was given a glimpse of my childhood past when I felt myself raising my right shoulder, hoping it would take the blow from Jackie's bat, instead of my head. I was all of three years old at the time.

Soon after that, I remembered my mom's favorite child-rearing tool for me: an 18" mahogany-colored bat, as you recall. The bat was thin, but extremely sturdy.

Her blows to my right shoulder and head happened so many times they had an effect on my posture as an adult. Sadly, I didn't know the reason why I rarely held my head up straight until after I did deep child within work.

Sometime later a friend of mine, Linda, introduced me to a brand-new concept for me. She helped introduce me to my inner child.

Linda was intuitive and knew there was more going on in my childhood that just a mean mom beating her three-year-old son with her favorite weapon.

Soon I had vague memories of being sexually assaulted as a child - beginning at age three. The perpetrators weren't strangers. I knew them all - and my dad, Jack, was part of their group.

Linda had a CD which I had never heard before, *Songs for the Inner Child* by Shaina Noll. The CD contains several songs which touched me so deeply that the tears flowed from the core of my being each time I heard them.

The first time I heard the song *How Could Anyone,* written by Libby Roderick and sung by Shaina Noll, I lost buckets full of tears, crying inconsolably.

By this time I was working with one, and then another, psychological counselor in Tyler. Neither was a survivor of abuse.

I didn't make much progress with either of them, though I gave it my best.

By then, my child within was screaming for help. I didn't know which way to turn or why. Church services in the Episcopal Church weren't providing the answers or solutions I needed. I don't believe there's any church in our country that could have.

The next year, I met Judy Goodman in her hometown of Columbus, Georgia. Her teaching is beyond conventional wisdom.

I'll always remember what Judy told me in that first meeting

"Jackson, you are the most energetically dead person I've ever seen alive."

Back then, I was so solidly entrenched in my left-brain way of thinking I thought such was a back-handed compliment.

Judy took me under her wing and saved me from what would have been certain death. A few years later I realized I was a dead person walking out his linear life. Before I met her, I was living on a thin sliver of life force, or as it is sometimes called, "borrowed time."

During my emotional recovery process, which includes working through physical, emotional, psychological, ritual and sexual abuse, I listened to songs and read the words from the inner sleeve of Shaina's CD many times. For years they continued to help me release even more buckets of tears.

Shaina's CD is still available for purchase from her website. For anyone who is now, or has gone through, the child within recovery process, I highly commend it to you.

Even if you only purchase the songs *How Could Anyone, It's a Joy to Get to Know You* and *Peace Be With You,* the songs are comforting and their lyrics are healing for your child within.

44

Challenge Your Beliefs

Most children absorb a lot from their parents. I certainly did.

Even after graduating from college, then law school and starting a family, I had the same values as my mom and dad had. I never questioned why I had the same religious beliefs, nor why I accepted their political views as being right.

If we are as smart as we believe we are in our Western culture, why do we have so many daunting problems that haven't been solved?

Somewhere in my recovery work, I decided to become myself instead of being my parents' puppet. I began exploring religions around the world.

A real eye-opener for me came from watching the movie *What the Bleep Do We Know?!* The main character was a divorced woman thrust into a world where science and spirituality converge.

Her concept of reality was challenged, just as I was challenging my own. The movie incorporated interviews with brilliant scientists, physicians, professors, a chiropractor and others. Each of them introduced a new concept for me to ponder. The movie was my first exposure to quantum mechanics, which scientifically is way outside my realm of expertise.

Just as I do when reading books, I incorporate what works for me and leave the rest behind.

It is a rarity for me, but I found it better to have watched the movie *What the Bleep Do We Know?!* before reading the book.

As for matters politic, I remember my dad and mom being huge fans of Barry Goldwater, the Republican Party candidate for president in 1964. They were certain he would lead our country into a new age of prosperity and cultural safety. My world view is quite different.

It wasn't until I became the mayor of my hometown that I discovered the truth about politics. It's a very ugly business.

Fortunately, I adopted a policy for myself when first elected. I quickly discerned that I lived in a fish bowl, with my actions visible and traceable to any who wanted to discover them, regardless of where I went or what I did.

For instance, a group of guy friends went to see a Notre Dame football game, each paying our own way. The surprise of the trip came at O'Hare Airport as we were heading home.

Out of nowhere came the words, "Hi Jackson." They were spoken by a female flight attendant who had grown up in Palestine and knew each of us.

Sadly, few politicians operate from a true heart-based premise. Instead, most do what they must in order to become elected or re-elected.

I knew during my second term that even I was tired of hearing my voice and that two terms in office was enough. It took time, but I was able to convince a well-known businessman in town to run for mayor in the next election. He would have carried the torch of community progress just as I had done my best to.

Less than two weeks before the filing window opened, the businessman, whose name is known only to me, called to let me know he wasn't going to run. I took the news in stride and decided there was too much at stake to let chance play its hand.

Our town was at the crossroads of change, once again. In the four years I had been mayor, we had cleaned up lots of messes and adopted business friendly policies.

Somehow, I eked out a victory over a virtually unknown opponent. I was grateful for the win, but was near burnout at that point.

During my tenure we were able to turn council meetings into business meetings. Unfortunately, I allowed the pendulum to swing too far in that direction, in hindsight.

Challenging my beliefs required me to find out what worked for me as well as what didn't. During this time, I read books on many different subjects.

Not only was I doing the child within work, but I also explored spiritual and religious books as well as matters metaphysical. The latter is merely the exploration of that which is not seen.

In one Frankie session, something profound happened. I let her know that I picked up on something she was carrying which could have dealt her body serious physical consequences.

Then I asked if she felt it, which she did. I asked permission to help her get rid of it, which she readily gave.

Asking for highest and best good, I focused on a spot on her chest and a hand position suddenly came to me. I didn't have a conscious thought about it.

After a minute or so, I was given a new hand position. The energy ran super-fast with the second one.

Frankie and I both felt something leave her body. I was super grateful she was able to rid herself of it.

Yet I was left with a mystery to solve. It took months for me to get a grasp of what was really happening.

I began working with the basic hand positions after work and spent hours trying to discern their meaning. In time I started writing a course manual.

Doing so required me to exit my left brained world and enter that of the right brain - a huge adjustment for me!

It took a few months, but I was finally close to the end of putting the course manual together. I recall being seated at my home-office desk in mid-December.

Without thinking, the fingers on my hand shifted upward by a single finger slot. Just this one change made me realize that the first hand position was like a house.

The new finger position led me to discover the neighborhood.

The first hand position clears energy from the emotional realm. Its counter hand position brings in energies for our highest and best good.

Working with our chakra system, that winter I discerned that each one has the same facets: emotional, mental, physical and the past.

Before I began the child within work, I had attended several seminars in which its leader would teach energy wellness techniques. Each one worked, but as I quickly learned, only for a short time.

What I learned for myself was that my healing requires digging out the psychological reason for the "dis-ease." Once that is known, the healing hand positions that I am a unique channel for in the world work their best.

Here I am - a lawyer, businessman and community volunteer. I encourage you to explore the unseen world to find your finest gifts, whatever they are.

**Be not afraid of criticism or condemnation.
Become the best you can be by challenging
yourself to awaken the soul within you that
sleeps.**

45

Women and Children
Are Our Equals

I was reared in a male dominated society. "The man rules the roost," is a common quote I heard umpteen times growing up.

Regardless of who is in charge, there is no excuse for abusing a child. My perception is that such abuse comes from a lack of parenting skills related to compassion.

I was spanked with the palm of my parents' hands. Friends of mine let me know their spanking was given by their dads who used their belts to whip them. I certainly felt sympathy for them as I bet a belt spanking hurt worse than a hand spanking, even when bent over my dad's knee.

"Spare the rod, spoil the child," is another quote I frequently heard growing up. I strongly believe in setting boundaries for children - with consequences. Somehow, we survived childhood, not knowing how our parents had imprinted us with their way of thinking.

I remember spanking my oldest daughter once. She was wearing Huggies diapers at the time. One swat was all it took as it made a loud noise which frightened her worse than the pop on her diaper-covered behind.

Where is it written that men are superior to women and children? I haven't found that written in any of the books I've read.

I remember early one morning a Baptist minister from another town wanted to know about an estate administration case I was handling. The only things I could tell the man was information that was in the court's file, which is a matter of public record.

At the end of the short meeting, the minister asked where I went to church. My truth, then and now, is what I told him.

"I go to church with every person with whom I have contact, whether by thought, word or deed," was my reply. The minister left my office in dead silence.

I bear the brunt of all my thoughts, words and actions. If they are wrong, I get to have them come back to me times seven, according to Judy Goodman.

Every man, woman and child is a child of God, who loves every one of us more purely than any human being ever could. We all carry that God seed within us.

Look closely into the eyes of another person. Focus on what you feel instinctively.

To look into the eyes of a child, do so by kneeling down so you are closer to being their height.

Truly our eyes are the windows into our soul.

For a number of years, I ran my law office and title company by pointing out to employees what they did wrong. That's how I was raised, but I shudder to think of the emotional damage I did to those employees.

Once I awakened to a new way of thinking, I began helping employees learn from their mistakes. I do so by helping them understand the reason they made the mistake. Then I give them some words of encouragement and empowerment.

The professional women whom I've mentioned in this book helped me in ways no man ever could. I am forever grateful to each one of them!

We live in a world that is changing faster than we can keep up with. In 2017, I mused that "life is relentless." Everyone I know confesses to feeling the same pressures to accomplish their daily tasks faster than ever before.

Even those of us who work from lists have had to adopt a new strategy. No longer can we work from a list all day.

Instead, we must modify our list hourly in order to stay on top of things.

By the first of 2018, I looked up from my crowded desk (which I refer to as "desk dunes") and also mused that life is now "relentless squared."

I humbly believe that in order to change the world for the better, we have to start with our own self.

It's only when I became an emotionally healthier person that I could help others improve themselves, too.

For some men, making the change to see women and children as our equal will require a substantial amount of inner work. Hopefully, for many others, it will come with ease.

46

Today Is What I Make Of It

From the moment I awaken, until the time I go to sleep, I have choices to make. As I go through each day, I usually come across people who are positive, those who are negative and those who are realists.

My good friend, Charlene Mayfield, reminded me of an important lesson in life years ago. At the time, I was taking group ballroom dance lessons from an instructor in Tyler.

One of her students suggested I contact Charlene, who was then teaching in Jacksonville, Texas, and take a lesson from her. I decided to give her a call as Jacksonville was closer to where I live.

My previous instructor had allowed me to lead with my left hand, which to Charlene's way of teaching was a huge no-no. For the first three private lessons, Charlene had me lead her with only my right hand and had me put my left hand in my rear pocket.

It was very awkward at first, but then I began realizing the importance of what Charlene was teaching me on how to lead a lady on the ballroom dance floor. The communication from my right hand to my dance partner's left shoulder is very subtle.

The analogy I have come up with is that leading with my left hand is akin to leading your dog on a leash. With that understanding, I certainly realized why my dance partners preferred that I lead with my right hand.

Charlene had just gone through a tough divorce and was a single mom raising her teenage son, who was acting out his frustrations and rebellion in ways that challenged her.

As tough as what Charlene faced with her son was, she never once shamed him or blamed him. Yes, of course, she gave him consequences for his juvenile mistakes.

It would have been normal in our culture for Charlene to have groaned and moaned about her woes with him, yet she never complained once. Instead, she viewed her son as her teacher.

The invaluable lesson that Charlene taught me by example was always to find the good in whatever situation you face.

Since then, I've faced numerous opportunities in life.

In the spring of 2018 we had several inches of rain in two days.

The opportunity I had at my law office was a stream of water flooded down the east side of the building. The leak came about because the outside electrical outlet lost power for some reason, so the sump pump connected to it never turned on.

Then the next day, I found termites inside my house. A day later an exterminator treated for them and showed me the damage they had done.

Sometimes we need wisdom from others to understand why things happen. In the Native American culture, totems appear and are to be paid attention to, as they are messengers.

Renee Bouma let me know that termites, like ants, represent team work, persistence, and everyone working for the good of the whole. Yet termites to Renee also represent something attacking the foundation of what I was trying my best to create.

The water coming into the building represented a spiritual blessing in disguise. I believe Renee's assessment was spot on.

Yes, the water flood caused disruption in the office. Loud fans blowing air to dry out the carpet, plus the noise of tearing out some sheet rock and removing some baseboards. In short order the water damage was repaired.

The opportunity I faced was solving how to redirect the water away from the north (back) side of my building, as it collected on the concrete slab where the dry cleaner's washing and drying equipment once was. I had a cement dam poured to protect the soft bricks from the weight of water. Next, I'll have a second and more powerful sump pump installed.

The cure for the termite damage required replacing a bit of door facing and sheet rock in a closet. Yet the real solution was to seal up the small crack the exterminator found in the foundation. I had no idea it existed at the time.

In our culture most would complain about the woes of having to repair home and office at the same time. In fact, most would complain about life being unfair and the like. I learned a long time ago that my complaints never once brought a solution to any opportunity I faced.

Whatever our mind focuses on tends to bring a result for us to deal with, so staying positive under all circumstances is my personal choice.

Charlene provided a life lesson reminder for me. I am super grateful for her friendship and wisdom.

There is more power in being positive than we give credence to. What happens in our lives often follows our thought patterns.

Indeed, today is what I make of it. I choose to find the good in all experiences and to learn their meaning.

I am grateful to my most recent teachers, the termites who came into my house, and the water which came into my office. It is only when I understand the invisible reason something happens in my life that I can address my part of why it happened.

47

Cut the R&J

The phrase "rationalization and justification" may be new to you. It was while doing my child within work that it finally made its way into my life.

I was taught not to make excuses for whatever mistakes I made as a child. Mom was a stern taskmaster and Georgia, her housemaid, was the same too.

Georgia was allowed to keep a switch, which she used on me, on top of the refrigerator in the utility room. The switch was a small but live branch from an elm tree.

She made certain hers was always fresh, so it was more pliable and delivered more impactful blows when used.

I remember getting whelps on my calves plus stinging blows to my shoulders when I failed to meet Georgia's expectations. Once punishment was administered, I'd be sent to my room where I'd cry until remorse and regrets arose.

When allowed out of my room I would make my apologies, which were usually received coldly by my punisher.

Georgia was the perfect surrogate house-rule enforcer for Jackie when she was away. If I failed to meet their standards, Georgia would tattle on me to her.

Both women made my corporal punishment more severe if they discovered I didn't tell the full truth the first time. It took a while, but finally I surrendered, learning to tell the truth by age four, as if I were a responsible adult.

The first experience I remember of being on the receiving end of rationalization and justification came when I was in junior high school. Though just a bench warmer on the seventh-grade basketball team, I was given one opportunity to travel with the team to an away game on the bus one fall afternoon.

Jackie was out of town, but she arranged for someone to take me to back to school at the appointed time. That person, who didn't show up until an hour after the team's bus had departed, came armed with excuses - which are appropriately called rationalization and justification.

Emotionally, I was crushed. Yet in the big scheme of life, it was just the lesson of invalidation, which I had no clue existed at the time, showing up for me at an early age.

As a young child, I learned that it was more important for me to be honest with myself and others, and take the consequences, rather than try to justify my behavior by making excuses.

Being truly honest and accepting responsibility for my actions helps me become my authentic self. Plus, it makes me accountable to myself and others.

In my recovery work with Sara, I learned that rationalization and justification are excuses.

Rationalization and justification (excuses) are tools our egos use to mask feelings of inferiority and insecurity.

I would much rather be told someone's truth and deal with whatever the consequences are, as I know I can handle the truth. It is much simpler than having to search for truth in the forest of someone's rationalization and justification.

It is time for me to ditch my fear of hurting someone else's feelings and simply be authentically direct with them.

48

My Sophomore Upchucks

As a sophomore at the University of Texas, life was good. I had made it through my freshman year at the university with good grades.

On Friday evenings, I enjoyed going with friends to Mi Casa es Su Casa. The English translation of the restaurant name is "My House is Your House." It was a well-known and very popular Mexican restaurant near the University of Texas campus in Austin when I was an undergraduate student there from 1970 to 1974. They have a different location now.

We'd order a pitcher of beer to share among us as that was much cheaper than ordering single beers.

I enjoyed the cold, refreshing taste of the beer. Inevitably, after one beer and a single bite of Mexican food, I was off to the bathroom to toss my cookies (throw up).

That made no sense to my rational mind. I was relaxed and certainly not intoxicated. The same thing happened if I ever had a beer after consuming a mixed drink.

On one of my trips to spend the weekend at home, I made an appointment to see our family physician.

I had seen Dr. Don Carroll many times growing up. Back in 1969, I had signed up to take the fall offering of the SAT. It was one of the college entrance exams, which the University of Texas required.

My mom was a legacy there and my sister was already a junior at the university. Before my mom dropped me off, I told her I suddenly felt awful.

Not taking the exam that morning wasn't an option. I managed to get through it without falling asleep, somehow.

By the next day, whatever it was took my health downhill fast. All I wanted to do was sleep.

My throat burned when anything went down it. I was feverish, too.

On Monday, I awoke in a stupor, wondering why the sun was rising in the west. In fact, the sun was setting and I'd simply slept through the day.

During my appointment, Dr. Carroll told me I had many different things going on health wise in my body. According to him there was no single diagnosis. He said I had the symptoms of mono (mononucleosis), but others, too.

He prescribed Darvocet and a strong antibiotic. I was out of school for two weeks before I was strong enough to try even a half day at school.

I took the final exams late that semester. My teachers saw that I was in a weakened state, as I had lost fifteen pounds.

My expectation, as a college sophomore, was that Dr. Carroll would prescribe the solution for me. I will always remember that appointment with him.

Dr. Carroll asked how he could help me, as he told me I looked healthy. I told him what happened every time I ate Mexican food and drank a beer.

He had me lie down on his exam table, then turned his hands palms down and gently pushed deeply into my stomach area.

Dr. Carroll then quickly pulled his hands up. It made me feel that my stomach had been set on fire.

Asked how my stomach felt, I told Dr. Carroll that he'd set my stomach ablaze. I knew I was one step closer to the answer.

He then informed me that I had the beginning symptoms of having a full-blown ulcer. I had no idea.

What he told me next stunned me. He said that the problem I had was in my head, not in my stomach.

Then he related to me that when he was a freshman in medical school he had the exact same symptoms, and told me the advice his doctor had given him.

He was told that he was over-anxious and there was nothing a pill could do to stop it, as the solution to the problem was in his head.

That was the same advice Dr. Carroll gave me. At the time I wasn't interested in things like meditation or yoga. I shake my head at my shallowness back then.

It took several months, but little-by-little I improved. I first conquered my stomach's queasiness, reaching the point that I could drink a cold beer with my favorite Mexican food and keep it down.

With time, I could consume whatever foods and beverages I wanted to without throwing up.

Many years later, I gained a profound appreciation for Dr. Carroll's wisdom. Had he prescribed a pill for me, it would have masked my symptoms.

Instead, I found ways to calm myself and to relax in social settings. That was the solution for my college day throw-ups!

Dr. Lincoln (1991, 4th Rev. 2006, p. 608), in his book *Messages From the Body*, wrote about the root cause of ulcers. To paraphrase Dr. Lincoln, I had severe abandonment and betrayal feelings. I also had dependency and separation anxiety. Besides that, he wrote that I was desperate for mothering, but felt I had to earn it and that belief made me an achieve-aholic. He also wrote that I would try my damnedest to deserve the nurturing I so desperately desired, all the while feeling the load of excessive responsibility. The cause of all this having been from an anxious and catastrophizing family.

My parents had placed me in a position of responsibility that was way, way over my head.

49

Elbow Speak

By 2007 Texas First Title Company was bursting at the seams. We were using all of the available space in the building I have owned since 1981. It's a historic building on the courthouse square in Palestine.

I received word that the Paramount Cleaners building, just two doors east of the title company building, was going to be up for sale. Quickly, I decided to buy the building, find someone to renovate it, and then move my law office into it.

There were all sorts of hurdles to overcome after the earnest money contract was signed. The first one was a requirement that a Phase One Environmental Survey be done. I engaged a firm that does such work out of Tyler, Texas, and their survey found a small piece of pipe in the building that was asbestos covered.

The stunner was that they found where cleaning fluid had leaked out through the floor. I knew there were two kinds of cleaning fluids: toxic and non-toxic. Perchloroethylene (commonly called "perc") is toxic if spilled and could require remediation, which is very expensive.

The topography of where the building sits is interesting. Old timers told me for years that from the courthouse all water either drains to the east, west or south. Yes, it's on that sort of a hill.

At night my mind would wander all over the place as to which direction the cleaning fluids had gone plus how far they had traveled. Within a couple more weeks, as I grew more anxious daily, the Phase II report came in.

The cleaning fluid used was of the non-toxic variety. I breathed an enormous sigh of relief and my lender gave us a clear to close.

I had a bit of history with the lawyer who represented the owner of Paramount Cleaners. In 1991 he had hired my real estate closer and my legal secretary away from me. As I recall they gave me no notice.

At the time I was also the mayor of Palestine, which earned me a whopping two hundred dollars a month and required significant chunks of my time each day.

I was upset at my loss and took it really hard for a few days. Then it dawned on me - I had been given the chance to improve on what my office could do for my clients.

Sue Miles came to the rescue and filled the closer's position. It then took several years with numerous legal secretaries coming and going before a real jewel showed up.

Her name was Susan, from Jacksonville, Texas. Though her main background was family law, which I don't practice, I decided she was worth a try.

Susan was super organized, had been an office manager before, and had a great work ethic. We made a great team!

I closed on the building. Luckily, I located someone who hauled off all the old laundry presses out of the building for their scrap value. Bit-by-bit I was able to get the building gutted.

When it came time to make the decorating decisions, I took Susan with me. We went to hardware stores, lumber yards, our local Lowes, and to Tyler to find prints to hang in the new office. We also went to office furniture stores.

Susan and I clicked when it came to decorating tastes. She also was quick to agree or disagree, so shopping was fast and easy!

By the time the building was finished, we were super happy and proud of the way the new office looked. It was unique, and unlike most professional buildings, it feels like home when you walk in the door.

Several months before the building process was completed I had begun bumping into walls at the title company. I was hitting the hall walls with my right elbow. This was odd for me, as I've always been nimble, thanks to my childhood. Whenever my elbow hit the wall it created a surge of searing pain through my right arm.

As the months wore on, it also became painful to shake someone's hand, so much so that within a couple of months I would grimace internally and steel myself for what was to come.

I still smiled with my handshake, so no one could suspect what I was feeling. Internally, though, I utterly dreaded handshake opportunities.

It was time to find some wisdom from Dr. Michael J. Lincoln's incredible book *Messages From The Body*. On my first attempt to find out what was causing my physical pain I looked up elbows.

Unfortunately, the root cause of elbow pain didn't come close to fitting either the history I had or the circumstances of the past year. I sighed and kept on going.

Two more months went by with no relief. Instead, the sharp bolt of pain that came from my elbow hitting the walls kept increasing in intensity and continued to become more painful with each handshake.

In retrospect, it would have been wise for me to make an appointment to see Edith Mitchell, then Frankie Burget. Instead, I kept moving forward, as each day had important tasks to be completed and I thought I was too busy to go see them.

A couple of months later I took the time to read what Dr. Lincoln had to say about joints, as my elbow fit that category. Unfortunately, there wasn't a hit with his diagnosis of the root cause of joint pain, either.

By August, which was two months later, the pain was still increasing in intensity. So much so, that I considered making an appointment to see an orthopedic surgeon in town. Cutting off half of my right arm at least would stop the breathtaking bolts of pain shooting through it.

Finally, I decided to give Dr. Lincoln's book one more try.

The only other body part I could think of that might fit was the arm (1991, 4th Rev. 2006, p. 79). I read what he had to say about the emotional root cause of arm pain and was shocked!

It was as if Dr. Lincoln had been following me around for the previous year and a half as I dealt with the excruciating right arm pain. One of the comments he made was, "They are having difficulty in manifesting assertiveness and confidence. They are feeling like... they really don't know what they are doing..." He was so on point that eighty-five percent of the pain disappeared immediately!

With one therapeutic massage, the rest of the right arm pain left my body for good. I was extremely grateful for the massage therapist's wonderful work. She also got my body to release some shoulder triggers that had had their start in childhood.

Yes, of course they came from Jackie's favorite weapon to use against my childhood body - the mahogany bat.

I can overcome my childhood past by doing the work to gain an understanding of its impact on my adult mind and body.

For as long as I am alive I will continue with the Edith, Sara and Frankie appointments. I'll do everything possible not to carry one bit of my childhood horrors across the veil of death when I die.

50

Setting the Table

Setting the table in my generation of baby boomers meant exactly that. As children, most of us learned how to set the table with proper silverware, glassware and napkins. Sadly, in these times most families in our country don't even gather as a unit to share meals. We're all busier than we've ever been in our lives and each of us has our own agenda.

When our youngest daughter, Lucy, was five, we sent her to Tyler with a friend of hers to take a class taught from the book of *Miss Manners' Guide to Excruciatingly Correct Behavior*. Both girls enjoyed their day.

Early that evening, as our family meal was winding down, Lucy put her silverware on her plate. I chuckled to myself as she set her knife and fork as if her plate was a clock that had just struck four.

I asked her what she was trying to do. She replied that they had been told to put their silverware at four o'clock when they finished their meal.

I was told the same thing growing up, but the silverware is supposed to be placed as if the time were really 4:20. Sometimes grownups need to be more specific with their children.

Years later, as Lucy was in high school, I deeply admired her volunteer service. What she did will always impress me. It was a couple of years after the divorce of myself and her mother that Lucy decided to spend a summer with me in Palestine, Texas, her hometown.

Within days, my daily requirement was to have her at the local hospital's emergency room before seven each morning, as she was too young to drive herself. I was to pick her up when she called me, which was rarely before seven p.m.

I was later told, by nurses I knew at the hospital, that as a volunteer she did the grunt work which no one else liked to do. My daughter lapped it up and just kept on going day after day. Like a true professional, getting her to talk about her day just didn't happen.

She spent each of her successive high school summers with me until she graduated, plus some weekends and a bit of time at holidays. Over the course of four years she put in over twelve hundred service hours in the local emergency room. Most of us in our lifetimes will do less than that in all the charitable service organizations we serve.

At graduation she was honored by her high school in Bedford, Texas, and given two significant awards for it. She received the Community Service Award and Christian Service Award at her senior awards assembly.

The Mother Teresas and Florence Nightingales of the world give of themselves freely. They understand the reasons why. In addition to helping those in dire need of assistance, they give their glowing light and love to those whose paths they cross.

Service to mankind is not for the accolades. It is for the self-satisfaction that you have given freely of your time to help someone who, for whatever reason, could not help himself or herself at that moment, with no expectation of receiving a thing or so much as a simple "thank you."

Those who give of their time from their hearts are the backbone of what is good and decent about mankind. They teach us by example, showing us how to pay it forward.

On a larger note, the society we live in is the product of former generations of adults setting the table for us. Whether we like the social trends and where our country stands with morals, domestic violence, school shootings and more, they have all been put into place by preceding generations.

In my legal profession, I prepare estate plans for clients. With only folks with great wealth facing estate and inheritance death taxes in place now, I've changed the label to more accurately reflect one area of my law practice.

Now I help clients with their legacy planning. Every one of us will leave a legacy when we die.

There is so much that can be done to improve the way things are now. Schools need after hour volunteers. The elderly in extended-care facilities could use a kind hand to just let them know someone cares about their wellbeing.

Our youth could be taught cursive writing in Texas, as sadly it isn't part of the Texas school curriculums any more.

How can we expect children to read ancient documents, such as the Declaration of Independence and our Constitution, if they can't write or read cursive text?

Of course, there are numerous factors and factions that have helped us reach the place where we are now.

Every one of us can do something. I believe it is our duty in this country to leave the world a better place to live in than the one we grew up in.

Please help set the table for our children and grandchildren. If every adult just does one unselfish act to help someone else less fortunate than they are, billions of children will be helped.

Your legacy lasts for generations.

The legacy of abuse, and that of a loving, caring, understanding upbringing, doesn't end with the death of the children's parents. Instead their parents' legacy lasts for several generations.

51

I'm Fine

Midway through my child within recovery work with Sara, my friend Linda asked me how I was doing one day. My response was my usual one then, "I'm fine."

Linda chuckled and then told me the true meaning of "fine." To her, when someone says they are fine it means they are "f***ed up, insecure, neurotic and emotional."

Shortly thereafter, I realized that I was at least three-fourths of what she said. Worse than that, I mused that I must be the president of the East Texas Chapter of Fine. I continued my intense work with Sara and with Frankie Burget, making headway. Healing all the layers of my emotional onion took time, determination, effort and patience.

Within a couple of months after Linda told me her meaning of fine, I went to Houston to attend a workshop hosted by Laura, an acquaintance. It was another of the energy wellness workshops that I felt could accelerate my emotional healing process.

As I drove in to Houston I had a chat with Laura. She had a great sense of humor.

She asked me how I was doing, and I told her that I had learned not to say, "I'm fine", thank you very much. Then she asked what the word meant to me.

I let her know what Linda had told me and Laura laughed hard. She then let me know that to her I had the meaning of "fine" all bucked up.

Fine to her meant that a person was "f***ing in need of everything." I acknowledged her wisdom by telling her how right she was.

I also let Laura know I was the proud president of the two chapters of "Fine" in East Texas. At least I could laugh at myself.

I knew I had to come up with a better response to use when someone asks me how I am doing.

The response I've used since then came to me quickly.

Now I say, "I'm doing well, thank you." So far it has stuck without my finding out I'm the president of another group of folks in desperate need of emotional recovery.

The emotional recovery process from all the categories of abuse I experienced as a child was messy. At least I figured out that net forward progress was normal.

Not only that, the process led me to folks who helped speed up my recovery. I'm grateful to Linda and Laura for their humor and wisdom.

Saying that I am well, when asked, has a deeper meaning to me than the superficial words. I truly mean what I say when I use that phrase.

After all, how I am faring emotionally after healing a multitude of layers of my "onion" is now a choice.

I rise above my temporary emotional setbacks.

That's because I recognize them as my teachers and am grateful for their appearance in my life.

52

I Choose

It would be easy to whine, bitch, moan and complain about what happened to me in childhood. You've read about the abuse I endured.

My mom was an excellent teacher for me, though. For several years before she died, I mused to others that she had PMS.

Most thought I had lost my mind, as that's a physical impossibility for a female in her eighties. I held my ground though.

To me, PMS meant "Poor Me Syndrome." Jackie was blessed with it in face-card spades.

She chose to see herself as a victim. True, she became a widow at an early age, but that is mere rationalization and justification for her behavior.

Once I began the journey of healing my life, I had many, many choices to make. The list below is not all-inclusive, but is a list of many I've made – and ones that you could, too.

I choose to be a survivor, not a victim. A survivor who endured and survived all that the perpetrators of abuse threw at me in childhood.

That's because God always gives me the strength to get through whatever I face. Yes, it may be emotionally painful, but it only brings me closer to my loving Mother/Father God.

I choose to love my Mother/Father God with all I Am, for She/He has always been there for me.

I choose to find the beauty in people, in nature, and in everything that happens to me.

I choose to love instead of hurting others.

I choose to be a guiding light so that others can find their way, wherever the streaming light and living force from God takes them.

I choose to let my childhood past teach me how not to treat others.

I choose to finish learning my unfinished lessons from childhood.

I choose to learn from those who appear in my life and those who depart from it.

I choose to be kind, gentle and gracious as much as I can be - to everyone.

I choose to set effective personal boundaries with everyone.

I choose to help others see how good they are.

I choose to help others find their hidden gifts.

I choose to help people understand the impact their thoughts and words have on themselves and others.

I choose to encourage and empower others to become the best they can be.

I choose to love and send appreciation to my angels, guides and masters who are always there for me - even when I feel the most unlovable.

I choose to set positive intentions for each day's outcome in my life.

I choose to become the best I can become.

I choose to follow my inner voice and guidance.

I choose to use positive words.

I choose to be authentic.

I choose to be passionate about living life!

I choose to take charge of my life and let my past be my teacher.

I choose to be mannerly to others - always.

I choose to be that gentle person people remember.

I choose to love myself in an emotionally healthy way.

I choose to find my faults and work to improve them.

I choose to have positive thoughts.

I choose to listen well.

I choose to be determined in all my endeavors.

I choose to be the best example possible for others to follow.

I choose to see the beauty in all God's creation.

I choose to remain calm at all times.

I choose to let my voice be heard.

I choose to be a man of peace.

I choose love over hate.

I choose gratitude over ingratitude.

I choose appreciation over disregarding.

I choose to bless instead of condemn.

I choose to encourage instead of discourage.

I choose to empower instead of destroying.

I choose courage instead of weakness.

I choose to ask for God's guidance daily.

Amen – and The End.

Recommended Reading

It Will Never Happen To Me! Claudia Black, Ph.D.
Facing Love Addiction: Giving Yourself the Power to Change the Way You Love, Pia Mellody
The Journey from Abandonment to Healing, Susan Anderson
One Soul, One Love, One Heart: The Sacred Path to Healing All Relationships, John E. Welshons
Transforming Fate Into Destiny, Robert Ohotto
Dare to Be Yourself: How to Quit Being an Extra in Other People's Movies and ..., Alan Cohen
Transforming Your Dragons: How to Turn Fear Patterns into Personal Power, Jose Stevens, Ph.D.
The Emotion Code, Dr. Bradley Nelson
Choose Them Wisely: Thoughts Become Things! Mike Dooley
I Don't Want to Talk About It: Overcoming the Secret Legacy of Male Depression, Terrence Real
The Five Love Languages: How to Express Heartfelt Commitment to Your Mate (Men's Edition), Gary Chapman
You Can Heal Your Life, Louse Hay
Feelings Buried Alive Never Die, Karol K. Truman
The Greatest Miracle in the World, Og Mandino
The Return of The Ragpicker, Og Mandino
Codependency for Dummies, Darlene Lancer

Heart Centered Music

How Could Anyone - Album: Songs for the Inner Child (Shaina Noll)

It's a Joy to Get to Know You - Album: Songs for the Inner Child (Shaina Noll)

Peace Be With You – Album: Songs for the Inner Child (Shaina Noll)

Angelic Love Section 1 – Album: The Silent Path (Robert Haig Coxon)

Angelic Love Section 2 – Album: The Silent Path (Robert Haig Coxon)

Finding Peace – Album: The Silent Path (Robert Haig Coxon)

Gabriel – Section 1 – Album: The Silent Path (Robert Haig Coxon)

Gabriel – Section 2 - Album: The Silent Path (Robert Haig Coxon)

The Light – Album: The Silent Path (Robert Haig Coxon)

The Silent Path – Section 5 – Album: The Silent Path (Robert Haig Coxon)

Toward the Light – Album: The Silent Path (Robert Haig Coxon)

Angelos - Album: Numinous (George Skaroulis)

Hopes and Dreams - Album: Generations (George Skaroulis)

Mythos - Album: Numinous (George Skaroulis)

Shenandoah - Album: Generations (George Skaroulis)

Anticipation – Album: Winter Poem (Secret Garden)

Atlantia - Album: Songs From a Secret Garden (Secret Garden)

Celebration - Album: White Stones (Secret Garden)

Hymn to Hope - Album: White Stones (Secret Garden)

Papillon - Album: Songs From a Secret Garden (Secret Garden)

Sanctuary - Album: White Stones (Secret Garden)

Song From a Secret Garden - Album: Songs from a Secret Garden (Secret Garden)

Song For a New Beginning - Album: Winter Poem (Secret Garden)

You Raise Me Up - Album: Once in a Red Moon (Secret Garden)

You Raise Me Up – Album: The Best of Secret Garden (Secret Garden)

Christmas Canon - Album: The Christmas Attic (Trans-Siberian Orchestra)

Bridget O'Malley - Album: Montana Skies (Montana Skies)

Once Upon a Time - Album: Atmospheres (Michael Dulin)

I Am Always Right Here - Album: Imaginations Light (Kevin Kern)

Imagination's Key - Album: Imagination's Light (Kevin Kern)

Pastel Reflections - Album: Summer Daydreams (Kevin Kern)

Safe in Your Embrace - Album: Imagination's Light (Kevin Kern)

The Enchanted Garden – Album: In the Enchanted Garden (Kevin Kern)

Touched By Love – Album: Walking in the Clouds (Bernward Koch)

Travel Lightly – Album: Walking in the Clouds (Bernward Koch)

In the Midst of Angels - Album: Angels in Solitude (Dan Gibson)

Voices of Peace - Album: Angels in Solitude (Dan Gibson)

This is Your Time - Album: This is Your Time (Michael W. Smith)

Reunion - Album: Streams of Light (John Astin)

The Elegance of Pachelbel - Album (Michael Maxwell)

Look Through My Eyes – Album: Brother Bear Soundtrack (Phil Collins)

You'll Be in My Heart – Album: Brother Bear Soundtrack (Phil Collins)

In the Mirror - Album: Love Songs (Yanni)

Nightingale - Album: Tribute (Yanni)

Flight of the Condor - Album: The Great Southwest (Nicholas Gunn)

South Rim - Album: The Music of the Grand Canyon (Nicholas Gunn)

Land of Forever - Album: Land of Forever (2002)

Somewhere Over the Rainbow - Album: Unspoken (Jim Brickman)

Night in That Land - Album: Shadow of Time (Nightnoise)

Time to Say Goodbye - Album: Time to Say Goodbye (Andrea Bocelli & Sara Brightman)

I Believe – Album: Songs of Inspiration and Praise (The Lettermen)

Brian's Song – Album: Brian's Song (Michel LeGrand)

What a Wonderful World – Album: What a Wonderful World (Louis Armstrong)

Bring Him Home – Album: Hits Volume 1 (The Piano Guys)

Like the First Day – Album: Twilight Time (Andre Gagnon)

Furusato – Album: World on a String (Daniel Kobialka)

Stella Maris – Album: The Sacred Well – The Best of 2002 (2002)

Summer of 300 Years - Album: The Sacred Well - The Best of 2002 (2002)

River of Stars - Album: Land of Forever (2002)

References

Covey, Steven. Brainy Quote - Retrieved May 18, 2018 from https://www.brainyquote.com/authors/stephen_covey

Emoto, Dr Masaru. 2004. *The Hidden Messages in Water.* Oregon: Beyond Words Publishing, Inc.

Frost Robert. Poetry Foundation Mending Wall- Retrieved May 18, 2018 from https://www.poetryfoundation.org/poems/44266/mending-wall

Lincoln, Michael J, PHD. 1991, 4th Revision 2006. *Top 50 Messages From The Body - Their Psychological Meaning: The Body's Desk Reference.* Spring Creek NV: Talking Hearts LLC.

Merton, Thomas. Retrieved July 16, 2018 from https://www.goodreads.com/quotes/351503-indeed-the-truth-that-many-people-never-understand-until-it

Oriah, The Invitation, Retrieved May 18, 2018 from http://www.oriahmountaindreamer.com/

Rand, Ayn, Retrieved July 16, 2018 from https://quoteinvestigator.com/2015/04/30/reality/

Book Acknowledgments

Thank you, Tom Bird, for being my "Book Whisperer." Your wisdom, suggestions and counsel helped more than any words I can say!

I am deeply grateful to Bill Worth, my first editor. Though I had to add another third to the book after his editing, his encouragement and stunning quote gave me the confidence to continue improving the book.

I send much gratitude to Denise Cassino for helping me with the many aspects of getting the book published that were out of my league. Most especially, though, for telling me to write another third beyond the manuscript she first saw.

Karen Collyer, warrior, survivor and my amazing second editor, took me under her wing, was always patient with me and honored my thoroughness.

She puts herself in the author's shoes to help the book become the best it can be! My words of deep gratitude and appreciation for her editing skills, graciousness and kindness aren't sufficient.

For me, she is the best editor I could possibly have worked with.

I am also very grateful to my proofreader, Janet Franecki. She caught the word hiccups that needed to be changed. Then she absolutely stunned me with her unsolicited quote.

To Tom, Bill, Denise, Karen and Janet, I am forever grateful to each of you. You let me know this book will help people in their journey, which is my heartfelt desire.

Each of you helped me find the inner courage to be out front and public about what very few men have the courage to talk about publicly: the impact child abuse had on their lives.

About the Author

Jackson Hanks is a former mayor of his hometown, Palestine, Texas, having served three terms in that capacity. During his tenure, he received the prestigious Road Hand Award from the Texas Department of Transportation.

Jackson is a board-certified lawyer in Texas, with specialization in Residential Real Estate Law and Farm and Ranch Real Estate Law. He also owns and manages Texas First Title Company, LLC.

In 2015, Jackson was selected by the Palestine Area Chamber of Commerce as the community's Citizen of the Year.

Jackson's business work does not define him. Nor do his efforts spent volunteering for non-profit organizations that work to improve the quality of life in the community.

Those who meet and work with Jackson learn he is an encourager who does his best to empower everyone to become their best.

The real work Jackson has done in his life is overcoming the horrific experiences of his childhood. He has worked with extraordinary practitioners to learn the lessons - the driving forces behind them, and has done the work to overcome them.

Jackson will likely tell you he has more work to do yet, but he does so with an open and willing heart, with absolute gratitude to his teachers, in all their forms.

Made in the USA
Columbia, SC
21 November 2018